Successful
Treasure Hunting

Successful
Treasure Hunting

Roger Johnson

ISBN 0 9506076 0 6

© Jeneva Marketing Limited 1978

Edited, designed and produced by Pam Darlaston

Typeset by Ronset Limited, Darwen, Lancashire
and printed in Great Britain by
A. Wheaton & Company Limited, Exeter
for Jeneva Marketing Limited
13 Marylebone Road, London NW1

Contents

Foreword

There is an old saying 'Where your treasure is, there will your heart be also'. Certainly most treasure hunters put heart and soul into their hobby!

What is it that is so fascinating about seeking buried treasure? Surely it is more than just the hope of getting something for nothing—those who have searched with a metal detector seriously realise how much painstaking work goes into it. No, the urge to search is something more intangible than that. Some desire, which we all possess in varying degrees, the search for the unknown or, if your research has been thorough, the search for the known. Inevitably, to do it well you must be both systematic and patient; you have to be methodical.

Taking up the 'sport' immediately opens wider horizons. History, especially local history, must be studied with the zeal of a detective and likely localities investigated. Suddenly you find that you are a student of archaeology and you acquire an insight into geology. You get out into the fresh air in your wanderings and with luck make direct contact with a long buried past.

I have often speculated on the possibility that the (golden) fleece was one of the earlier 'aids' for collecting alluvial gold from river beds. My fondest personal memory of prospecting for gold from river beds, before the advent of modern sophisticated electronic equipment, was of descending into the depths of the Callery Gorge in New Zealand's Westland in the depths of winter when the water was low. We had to prise the nuggets from fissures on the rock faces. If only we had had a good metal detector to locate the gold-bearing reef which must be somewhere near the headwaters, close to the glaciers, we might have been successful.

This book has a fund of information for the prospective treasure hunter. It reveals many of the pitfalls which one can encounter and I trust that like me you will find it packed with information and sound common sense.

Hamish MacInnes
Glencoe, Argyll

Introduction

The idea of treasure hunting has captivated us for centuries. The urge that prompted Long John Silver to sail to Treasure Island and expeditions to be raised to find the hidden hoards of the swashbuckling pirates of the Spanish Main finds its counterpart today in the treasure hunter armed with his or her metal detector.

What has caused the hobby to grow and almost explode to such an extent during the past decade or two? Two factors chiefly. Firstly, rapid developments in the field of electronics have done much to improve performance and detector design and manufacture in Britain, particularly in the past two years or so. Secondly, of course, the publicity which has surrounded some quite sensational finds in recent years has caused a great jump in demand. In fact, following one such find local stockists were quite unable to cope with it all. Nothing breeds success like success. Statistics can be bent and generally manipulated to suit one's purpose, but there is no disputing that the hobby is growing fast and that sales of detectors indicate something approaching a one hundred thousand ownership in this country now. In the USA, where the hobby is longer established, one in every eight families is reputed to own a metal detector. The estimated value of recoveries by detectors in the United Kingdom in the past few years is said to be in excess of five million pounds. Quite apart from this undeniable attraction, the hobby is getting thousands of all ages and types out into the fresh air at weekends and on holiday. Families too are becoming engrossed and fascinated. Clubs are being formed up and down the country and with them, of course, a greater

9

degree of responsibility and the recognition and practice of a code of conduct (see page 137).

In a recent programme on television owners of metal detectors were criticised by an archaeologist. One hears rumblings too of legislation being brought in to restrict our activities and moves to make it difficult to obtain a licence to operate a detector. Hopefully, these are merely the growing pains of a fast developing sport or hobby. There is plenty of room for both the professional, academic archaeologist and the amateur treasure hunter. There is a dividing line of course and there is a paramount need to respect the priorities of the former whose work is often of very considerable national importance. The need for a responsible approach is stressed in later chapters. The prime purpose of archaeology is to try to reconstruct history and not necessarily to look for buried metal objects. It is the natural fear that a site, which is usually painstakingly revealed layer by layer, could so easily be ruined by a hole-digging amateur that causes the aggravation.

For whatever reason you chose to look at this book and read this far, I hope the following chapters will encourage and assist you. Like most things in life, the more effort you put in, the more interest and enjoyment you will gain. You will make very many good friends through your involvement with the hobby, your interests will broaden and, whilst there are always disappointments, there will be much pleasure to come.

A vast amount of treasure still remains hidden from view. With the greatly improved equipment which is now available, you have far better prospects of finding it than ever before. Whilst your horoscope might indicate that lady luck is smiling on you, you will find that you will need patience and know-how to be really successful. You might well be one of those, however, who confound the pundits and hit the jackpot first time out with the cheapest model from the local shop! You never know . . .

1 Treasure Rediscovered

The Treasure Hunters Association of Great Britain has been quoted as saying 'We believe there is something like five hundred million pounds in lost or buried treasure in Britain alone'. This figure can, of course, only be inspired guesstimation, but with a history as rich as ours it could well even be a conservative estimate. We are hardly likely to see the kind of priceless treasures found in Egypt in the tombs of the Pharaohs or those attributed to the Aztecs or Incas, but nevertheless large numbers of caches must exist around the country which equal them in terms of historical and social interest.

Richard Davies, a travel agent from Buckinghamshire, is typical of the enthusiastic and dedicated but responsible amateur metal detector users who enjoy the hobby. He has many successes to his credit and in the autumn of 1975 found a rare William II penny a few inches below the surface of wooded scrubland near Gerrards Cross, Buckinghamshire. Because of its rarity the coin was donated to the British Museum who did not possess such a coin themselves. The penny is of the William II Type V of the Oxford mint but unfortunately, due to damage, it did not prove possible to identify the moneyer. However, comparisons with a similar coin in the Hunterian Museum at Glasgow University shows Mr Davies' find to be virtually unique, since it was struck from different dies. Another find was a David II silver penny which he unearthed in a friend's garden in Hertfordshire. Whilst not unique, it is a rarity and not listed. Elizabeth I is reputed to have stayed at this house, so it offers good promise for further finds. The illustration shows the superior quality of the

11

Richard Davies with the William II penny donated to the British
Museum

hammered portrait face which makes it very interesting.

'On average' Mr Davies says, 'I find one or two coins a month which are over two hundred years old. Among my finds are numerous Georgian coins, a shilling and copper coins of the seventeenth century.' Since taking up treasure hunting during the last two years or so, he has recovered a large number of coins, badges, musket balls, silver spoons, rings and other relics of times past. It is fair to say, however, that most of the coins are Victorian or modern. The depth at which a coin is found has little bearing on its age, he finds, and within a 200-square-yard area he has found coins from the fifteenth, six-teenth, seventeenth, eighteenth, nineteenth and twentieth centuries.

'Much of my success is due to research,' Mr Davies explains, 'comparing modern maps with the first Ordnance Survey maps published around 1822.' He finds that estate agents often supply maps of the locality which have excellent

The David II silver penny found by Richard Davies and donated to the Oxfam Coin Appeal 1977

detail. Other principal ingredients of success, he says, are 'luck, perseverance, imagination, intuition and good reliable equipment'.

Philip Connolly is one of the most consistently successful treasure hunters in the country. Hailing from Kent, Philip is something of a veteran at the game and over the years has amassed considerable experience and in consequence is a fascinating person to talk to. His first venture with a metal detector was in 1964, although he had been a keen amateur archaeologist for some time before this. His first detector, an ex-army valve mine detector, cost him £4 10s 0d and proved to be 'not much better than useless'. On his last trip out with it, it failed to detect a Roman copper coin which he actually saw lying on the ground, so it was promptly disposed of at a jumble sale for 1s 6d. Using his knowledge of electronics as a professional telephone engineer, he started to build a beat frequency detector; whilst it only showed a marginal increase of efficiency over the previous acquisition, it enabled him to grasp the fundamentals of his new hobby.

Reading an article in the local paper concerning the recovery of three thirteenth-century gold coins, Philip next invested in the purchase of an induction balance detector. This increased the scope of his finds to an average of ten coins an hour at times. His collection has included thousands of coins dating from Roman to modern times, as well as interesting artefacts, musket balls, badges, knives, rings, etc. He is a very painstaking and careful researcher and, as a result of three years of such research, he recently made his most significant find. This is how Philip recounted the story.

'After hearing a rumour of a boy finding a Roman coin by the edge of a road at Meopham in Kent, I began a systematic search of the area in the hope of finding a concealed hoard. The area was littered with junk, old iron and silver paper and thus I spent many hours fruitlessly digging up rubbish for the local scrap dealer! However, I had narrowed the possible site to a section of steep roadside banking. Deciding that the search merited a detector which offered above average penetration, junk rejection and automatic tuning, I decided to purchase an Auto Discriminator. I spent two evenings familiarising myself

Philip Connolly with two of his valuable finds

with the controls and the characteristics of the machine. On the Saturday, I then searched the local beach which I had already diligently searched with my previous detectors. In two hours I discovered two keys and twenty-one coins. On the Sunday I scanned a small section of the common and within one and a half hours I uncovered thirteen coins, three badges and an army button. I became so enthusiastic that on the Tuesday I searched an old camp in my lunch hour—the result another seventeen coins. On the following Friday I was working in the Meopham area and could not resist the temptation to put my theory to the test by searching the road banking. I began my search and twenty minutes later I unearthed six Edward III gold nobles, all of which were in superb condition. The coins were buried at a depth of only six inches by the root of a tree. I returned to the site on two subsequent occasions and found a further four gold coins including an extremely rare Richard II quarter noble.'

At the treasure trove inquest, Miss Archibald, a British Museum expert, told the seven-man jury that the find was probably a hoard hidden by a cautious traveller entering Meopham in the 1400s. The coins date from 1354 to 1399 and were of significant value at the time of their concealment, approximately fifty-five shillings, which, nowadays, would be worth between three to four hundred pounds. The numismatic value of the find easily runs into thousands of pounds. As the find was declared treasure trove, Philip Connolly was to receive the full market value, or the actual coins back, from the British Museum.

When asked the reasons for his success, Philip replied 'I have lived in the area all my life and have taken an active interest in its history. This enabled me to complete a thorough investigation before commencing the actual treasure hunt. I believe in spending a considerable time familiarising myself with the detector so that its operation becomes second nature.' He continued 'The most important advice I can give to a potential treasure hunter is to be sure to buy a well proven

16

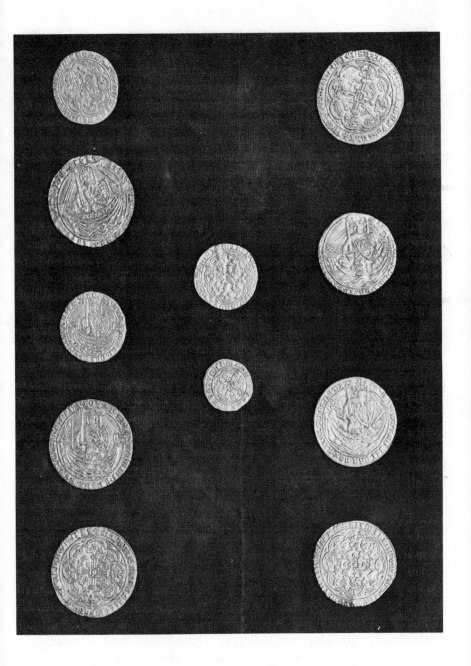

The seven Edward III nobles and three half nobles, and a Richard II
quarter noble found by Philip Connolly

17

brand of detector. There is nothing more frustrating than having to call off a hunt because the equipment has failed. Remember—do not ever ignore any informative signal, however faint—it might be the signpost to fame and fortune.'

Magnificent discoveries have been made over the years, some by archaeologists, some by amateur treasure hunters, some using painstaking scientific methods, some aided by the use of metal detectors and some, of course, purely by chance. Many treasures have been found and very many more remain to be discovered.

One of the most important finds in the last forty years was the discovery of the Sutton Hoo Burial Ship in 1938–9, found by the estuary of the river Debden in Suffolk. No body or human remains were found, but it is thought to have possibly commemorated King Redwald of East Anglia. A handbook on the project by Rupert Bruce-Mitford, MA DLitt FSA, keeper of the Medieval and Later Antiquities in the British Museum, makes fascinating reading and is a 'must' for all those interested in our early pagan history. Briefly, the site was an Anglo-Saxon burial ground of the sixth and seventh centuries at Sutton Hoo, just opposite the little Suffolk town of Woodbridge. Fourteen barrows, or burial mounds, were situated on land belonging to Mrs Edith May Pretty JP who, in 1938, decided to initiate a project and investigate their contents. Experts from Ipswich Museum and a local antiquary, Mr Basil Brown, were retained for the work and three of the mounds were opened, revealing much of interest, particularly relating to Anglo-Saxon burial practices. Unfortunately, due to ransacking, the finds were meagre but sufficient to prove the importance and status of the dead. One of the mounds had contained a small boat, but little remained of it due largely to destruction by the ransackers.

The pieces recovered, particularly from the one barrow which had apparently been left undisturbed and appeared to be an intact cremation, were sufficient to encourage further investigation in 1939 to open up the tallest of the barrows, one about nine feet nigh. Soon Mr Brown uncovered a system of rusted

The helmet of Swedish manufacture found among the Sutton Hoo ship burial treasure (*Mansell Collection*)

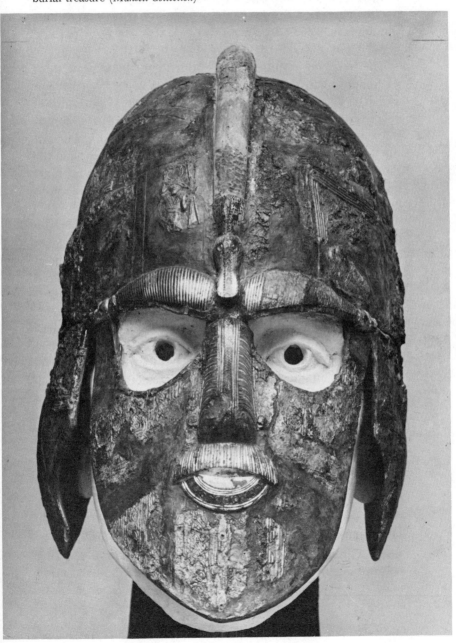

iron rivets which, from his experience of the previous year, could be attributed to a ship but of considerably larger size, probably up to eighty-nine feet long, the longest vessel yet found from the migration period or from the later Viking age. Its prow stood, in all probability, some twelve and a half feet high.

The remarkable thing is that the sea must have been all of six hundred yards away; the daunting task of moving the ship to its final resting place, up an escarpment, was doubtless effected on rollers. The burial chamber was constructed amidships, the common practice in Norwegian Viking ship burials; the burial deposit was then laid out and bracken strewn about. Finally the whole ship was buried in sand and a mound built up over the site. One can only imagine the very elaborate rituals that must have accompanied all this.

An attempt to ransack the mound was probably made in the sixteenth or seventeenth century, for a hole approximately ten feet deep was found, but fortunately it missed the burial chamber completely. To try to catalogue in a few hundred words the sheer scope of the modern excavation, the total dedication of those involved and the painstaking research which has continued to this day is impossible. The disintegration of the timbers over the centuries, leaving only rows of rivets in the sandy soil, meant a great deal of research into its construction. This, in conjunction with similar research in Scandinavia, has produced much vital and interesting evidence to substantiate previous theory, particularly in ship construction, in the sixth century.

The excavators, realising that they were about to make a discovery of supreme importance when they reached the centre of the ship where the burial chamber was expected to be found, felt it would be wise to call for expert assistance which was readily forthcoming. No one had ever excavated such a unique and important burial deposit in this country before. It was thought at first that the burial must have been that of a Viking because of similarity with burials in Scandinavia of the ninth and tenth centuries. With the recovery of the treasure, how-

A purse-lid made in East Anglia from the Sutton Hoo treasure (*Mansell Collection*)

ever, it soon became obvious that the burial belonged to an earlier age and was quite without parallel in British archaeology. There, buried in varying degrees by the collapse of the burial chamber, were gold jewellery, coins, silver plate, weapons and bowls, the remains of cauldrons, buckets and dishes of bronze and iron, textiles and leather drinking horns and miscellaneous other items. Altogether it was the richest and the most significant treasure ever found in the United Kingdom and of enormous importance in documenting the era of migration of the Germanic peoples in the sixth and seventh centuries.

In August 1939, a coroner's inquest was held to decide whether or not the items discovered were treasure trove. The coroner found that they were not and were therefore the property of the landowner, Mrs Pretty, who wisely and generously donated the whole of the find to the nation. Shortly afterwards, World War II broke out but the finds were already in the safe hands of the British Museum for careful restoration. The indescribable beauty and quality of workmanship must be seen to be believed and the burial has yielded examples of craftsmanship at the highest possible level. The tremendously wide range of the objects recovered, as well as their condition, make it 'the most marvellous find in the archaeological annals of England'. It is almost unbelievable that contacts with the Far East, as well as all round Europe, could exist in those far off days, yet the contents of the burial chamber revealed Frankish coins, pieces of Eastern silver, the Coptic Bowl from Alexandria, Celtic bowls, Swedish treasures and heirlooms and garnets originating from India. Such was the scope and influence of Anglo-Saxon royal court at the time. The restored pieces are on view in the British Museum and at Ipswich.

The enormous value of such archaeological projects in helping to determine the historical development of our nation and of mankind generally is incalculable and requires expertise and integrity of the highest order. Note particularly the decision in 1939 to call in more expert help when it was thought the discovery of something really important was imminent. Note too the decision of Mrs Pretty, even though the coroner declared the finds not to be treasure trove and therefore hers, to present it all to the nation.

A contemporary find was made with a metal detector by Mr Holbrook. It is a sixth-century Anglo-Saxon brooch, described

Mr Holbrook's sixth-century
Anglo-Saxon brooch

A Bronze Age sword hilt
found by Mr F. W. Hughes

by an assistant keeper at the British Museum as being in
remarkable condition and of a particularly interesting construction. It is made of silver gilt with garnet settings and a
black niello border, with stylised bird motifs between the

garnets. Mr Holbrook is a careful and responsible metal detector user, who co-operates fully with his local archaeological society. On the same hillside site where the brooch was found, Mr Holbrook also discovered an Anglo-Saxon shield boss and two ring brooches. The archaeological society has carried out a preliminary excavation but, as no further evidence has been discovered, it is thought that it may have been the site of a lookout or a tribal skirmish.

An even earlier find was made by Mr F. W. Hughes of a Bronze Age sword hilt. Because of discolouration and dirt he did not realise its full importance at first but did suspect that it might be made of bronze. He consulted a book on archaeology and found a photograph of something virtually identical—a late Bronze Age carp tongue sword, probably about 3500 years old. Now on loan to the British Museum, it is being studied to ascertain the metal content. The rivets which had secured the wooden handle were also discovered.

Whilst Sutton Hoo is of outstanding interest, many other important finds have been made in the United Kingdom. One

Two magnificent platters from the Mildenhall Roman silver plate hoard (*British Museum*)

of these was in 1876 when nearly twenty thousand coins, jewels, brooches and pots of different kinds were found in what was thought to be a sacred well near Hadrian's Wall and a temple of Mithras, an ancient god. Another Anglo-Saxon burial mound was discovered in a churchyard at Taplow in Buckinghamshire where there was a considerable find of gold jewellery. A number of Viking hoards of plunder have been found including one in Lancashire where a large cache of silver and coins were discovered.

The famous Mildenhall treasure discovered in 1946 contained priceless items of Roman silver, some of which bore great similarity to a looted hoard found in Scotland. The most impressive piece is a dish weighing over eighteen pounds, beautifully embossed with a mask of a sea god with a beard of seaweed and four dolphins swimming out of his hair; it is further adorned with other sea creatures and maidens, with an outer ring of figures taking part in a Bacchic dance, all pagan subjects. Coins found with the treasure were dated around AD407 and also discovered were bowls, platters, goblets, ladles and spoons. The spoons, because of their inscriptions, are of particular interest to the historian and can be seen in the British Museum. The estimated value of the treasure in 1946 was £1,000,000; the farmworker who discovered the hoard while ploughing was not particularly interested in the find; the farmer thought it was pewter and did not declare it. As a result, when it was declared treasure trove, the finders only received a token of £1000 each instead of the full value because the find was not declared immediately. The implications of treasure trove law are fully explained in Chapter 10.

Jim Smith, a detector dealer in Glasgow, gets great interest and pleasure from the hobby. The part of the country in which Jim lives is, of course, rich in history and many civilisations have left their traces. Probably his most interesting find is a bronze statuette believed to be of Graeco-Roman origin dated circa 500BC–AD200, thought by the Hunterian Museum to represent a male god, perhaps Apollo. It has not proved possible to be more precise but the British Museum has confirmed these main findings.

Jim had been searching an area in the vicinity of Kirkintilloch, near to the line of the old Antonine Wall. This was a Roman frontier barrier running between the Clyde and the Firth of Forth and was built around AD142 by Lollius Urbicus, the Governor of Britain at the time, on the orders of the Emperor Antoninus Pius. However, the revolt in the north in AD155–8 interrupted occupation of the wall and by AD196 it had been evacuated.

It took almost a year's searching before Jim made his discovery. His attitude was philosophical and after finding the odd Roman bronze coin or two he knew it was largely a

A bronze statuette thought to be of Graeco-Roman origin found by Jim Smith

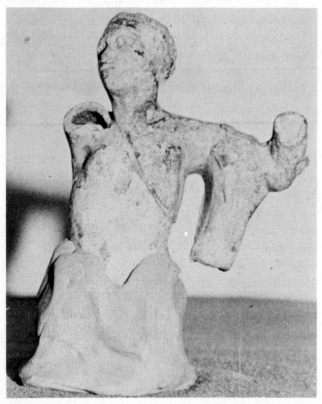

Controversy surrounds the identification of this gold coin found by
Jim Chapman

question of patience. When he eventually unearthed the
statuette, it was only three or four inches below the surface.
The reading on his discriminator model was not particularly
positive and he rather expected to find nothing more exciting
than the usual bottle top but, because he believes you cannot
afford to disregard any signal however faint, he decided to
investigate. Unfortunately the statuette is slightly damaged but,
considering its great antiquity, it is in generally good condition.
The material is Roman bronze which is not unlike pewter in
colour and texture.

Occasionally, of course, the origin of finds causes controversy
and speculation, with even the experts failing to reach agreement or any satisfactory conclusions. Such a find was unearthed
by Mr Jim Chapman near his home at Sandy in Bedfordshire
a couple of years ago. It is a gold coin bearing a mule and stars
pattern and is approximately one centimetre in diameter. The
British Museum have been very cautious in their assessment
and other experts are equally puzzled. The coin was at first
thought to be a Gallo-Belgic stater by the finder; these were

coins brought into Britain by immigrating tribes coming from Western Europe. One opinion has suggested that it might be a fake; but it could well be unique, and if it is proved genuine, probably belongs to the period 20BC to AD20. In this event it might well have been minted for the Catuvellauni tribe which inhabited central England at this time. Another archaeologist has suggested an earlier period and that the coin could have originated at Verularium (St Albans) where the royal mint of Tasciousenus, Chief of the Atrebates, was sited around 100BC. And so the argument and speculation goes on. Mr Chapman is very pleased with his find, however, and he is quite certain it is a very rare coin and he cannot wait to see it catalogued.

At the other end of the scale from Sutton Hoo is the amusing story concerning Mr F. Wiggs from the Kings Lynn area. After receiving his shiny new metal detector, unpacking it and carrying out some rather perfunctory trials, he shot off in his car to make his first fortune. He had already decided where to go, choosing an old Roman road as a likely source of new-found wealth! Arriving at his destination he parked his car, got out his detector, adjusted the headphones and started a textbook search. He began at the end of the broad path which was the site of the old Roman road and began working his way slowly backwards and forwards. Mr Wiggs had not been searching for too long before a very strong signal manifested itself and the needle swung over violently. He dug down with the trowel and found . . . a bottle top. Roman? Well you never know, he thought, and put it in his pocket. Silver paper! The Romans must have thrown an enormous amount of it away—it was everywhere! His worst problem, however, was a will o' the wisp signal which came in very strongly and then, unaccountably, would disappear without trace. This went on and on and finally, in sheer disgust, cursing the Romans, the manufacturers of the detector and the elusive signal, he packed up and went home. 'Still' he continued, 'I had my first find—a Roman aluminium screw top which still has pride of place on my display unit. I sank wearily into my armchair and bent down to undo my boots. Steel toecap working boots! These boots that had led me a merry dance all over the Roman road. They were sent crashing into the corner, never again to accompany me on a treasure hunting expedition.' So ended Mr Wiggs' first trip, and a valuable lesson learnt, fortunately without damage to his enthusiasm. A sense of humour certainly helps.

So one can go on! Treasure there is and a great deal more there must be waiting to be discovered and to see the light of day again, perhaps after centuries of concealment. Nothing has been mentioned of the priceless treasures of the Incas and the Aztecs plundered by the Spanish, or of the fabulous Tutankhamen. They belong to another world. It is a fascinating thought however that there, perhaps, not far from where you are situated at this very moment could be a hoard worth—well, who knows what.

2 What is a Metal Detector?

Whilst millions have successfully learned how to drive their cars without much knowledge of the forces that cause the wheels to turn, there is little doubt that such knowledge does help a driver appreciate the car's limitations and the way it can best be used. A metal detector is like any piece of equipment; a higher degree of performance can be achieved with it if the operator has a basic knowledge of why and how it works in addition to an appreciation of the value of certain features.

When buying a detector, the purpose to which it is to be put and the individual who is to use it must be considered. The weight, size, ease of use and metal-detection ability have to blend into a detector so that it fulfils the needs of the operator. In this chapter, in broad terms, are outlined how the various types work and the points to look for when buying your first detector. Firstly, we should consider the physical attributes of a good detector and the need for them (Fig 1).

Handiness

The weight and balance of a detector are perhaps the most important physical features. If the detector is incorrectly balanced and excessively heavy, the operator will not only find it necessary to curtail the search to the length of time his arms can bear the strain of swinging a cumbersome instrument, but also the discomfort caused will weaken the concentration necessary to detect finds at their maximum depth. A detector should be light and, when held correctly, balance naturally in the position in which it is to be used. In the early days, treasure

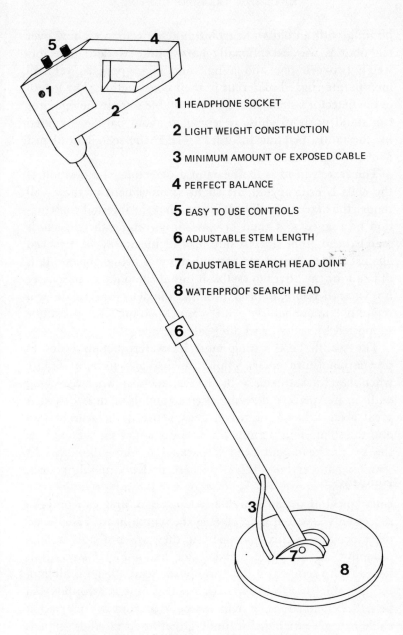

1 HEADPHONE SOCKET

2 LIGHT WEIGHT CONSTRUCTION

3 MINIMUM AMOUNT OF EXPOSED CABLE

4 PERFECT BALANCE

5 EASY TO USE CONTROLS

6 ADJUSTABLE STEM LENGTH

7 ADJUSTABLE SEARCH HEAD JOINT

8 WATERPROOF SEARCH HEAD

Fig 1   The physical features of a well designed metal detector

hunting with an old war surplus mine detector weighing over ten pounds was exceptionally hard work. Modern detectors weigh between one and a half and eight pounds, yet still incorporate rugged materials in their construction. The length of the detector's stem should be adjustable so that the operator can stand upright whilst sweeping to avoid backache caused by constantly bending in order to keep the search head just above the ground.

The search head is the heart of a detector. The position of the coils is critical and the slightest movement of these will render the detector useless. It is vital that the internal construction be rugged and rigid because, in sweeping the detector's search head from side to side, it will inevitably be knocked against stones, tree roots and other unforgiving objects. It is difficult for the buyer to establish this at the point of purchase; it is wise, therefore, to be certain that the detector is made by a reputable manufacturer who offers a no-quibble guarantee supported by a first class after-sales service.

The search head casing must be waterproof in order to prevent moisture entering and causing an electrical failure when searching streams or by the sea, and also when searching with an inexpensive detector after a rainfall or heavy dew. A great asset is having a swivel joint between the search head and the stem. This permits the operator to adjust the angle of the search head and keep it parallel to the ground whilst searching under low obstacles where finds frequently collect. Excessive pressure, in the case of fixed head detectors, can cause the top of the search head to crack and can only be successfully repaired by replacing the search head. Fixed head detectors are usually cheaper but they are probably a false economy. If, however, the detector has a metal stem, it is necessary to retune it if the angle of the search head is altered.

The cable that links the search coils to the control box can be either enclosed in the stem or wound around it. An external cable can get entangled in undergrowth or cause false signals if it becomes loose and flaps against the stem in the wind.

The tuning controls should be simple and accessible, so positioned as to prevent them being knocked out of tune during the sweep by the operator or by an obstacle such as a bush. Detectors which have the controls mounted either in the handle or on the front panel are very satisfactory.

How a Metal Detector Works

Despite their technical complexity, electronic metal detectors are based on a few simple principles discovered well over a century ago. The most important is the principle of electromagnetic induction. Stripped of jargon this means quite simply that if an object is placed in a changing magnetic field, an electrical voltage is created in the object. In metal detectors a changing magnetic field is produced by an electromagnetic coil. Passing a current through a coil of wire creates a magnetic field, so if a constantly changing current is passed through the coil the result is a constantly changing magnetic field. This changing field creates voltages in any objects which come within its influence.

If the objects are made of metal and therefore good conductors of electricity, the voltages induced into them by the field of the coil drive currents round and round inside the objects. To make the effect useful as a means of detecting a metal object, it is necessary somehow to detect the presence of these induced currents. This is the essential function of most of the complicated electronic circuitry of a metal detector.

So far, then, we have a coil of wire, to produce the necessary magnetic field; this coil is called the search coil. To produce the necessary changing field the coil is driven by a changing current, generally produced by a search oscillator—that is an electronic alternating current (AC) generator whose job is to convert the direct current (DC) from the battery into the AC needed to drive the coil. As AC regularly reverses direction, the required ever-changing magnetic field is created. Currents are induced in any metal object which comes within this magnetic field; to detect the object we have to detect the currents.

The trick is to make use of the fact that the process works in reverse. The currents in the object in turn produce their own magnetic fields. These fields are capable of inducing voltages in nearby objects, one of which is of course the search coil itself. The currents in the target object—say, a buried coin—react with the coil. The whole art of metal detector design is to sense this reaction. Fortunately it is now possible, thanks to the transistor and the integrated circuit, to pack all the necessary circuitry into a relatively small and light instrument.

Pulse Induction (PI)

The easiest kind of metal detector to understand is the pulse induction type of detector. In this the search coil is energised very briefly by a powerful current from the battery, then switched off. The resulting pulse of magnetism causes currents to start flowing in any target objects which happen to be around. But the current in a target cannot be switched off; it has to die away naturally, and is still dying away long after the current in the search coil which produced it has been switched off. This dying-away target current induces a voltage in the now inactive search coil. This voltage is amplified and made to give an indication to the user—a sound in earphones, a flashing light, a meter-pointer movement.

So the PI metal detector works by carrying out a sequence of operations. In the transmit or energise phase it creates the necessary magnetic field; in the switch-off phase it suppresses this field; in the receiving or listening phase it watches for the after-effects of the transmit phase, in the form of dying magnetic fields from target objects. These dying fields are often extremely weak. The voltages they induce in the coil are so small that it may be necessary to amplify them 100,000 times to make them produce a perceptible indication to the detector user.

Induction Balance (IB)

If a second coil is placed near the search coil, then this second coil becomes in effect a target object and a voltage is induced in it. The induction balance detector depends on the fact that this process does not always happen. It is possible to make coils of special shapes and place them in special positions near one another in such a way that the field of the transmit coil does not induce any voltage into the other (receive) coil (Fig 2).

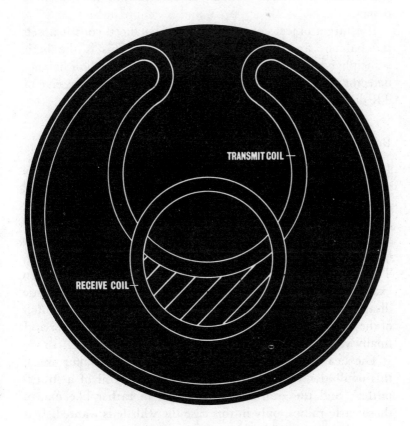

TRANSMIT COIL

RECEIVE COIL

Fig 2 The coil arrangement of an IB detector; the shaded section represents the area of highest sensitivity

In reality, of course, voltages *are* induced in the receive coil, but there are two voltages and they act in opposition to one another; when the size and shape and position of the coils are just right, this opposition is exactly equal and the two voltages cancel each other out, leaving nothing. The coils are then said to be in a state of balance—and it is a very delicate balance indeed. The slightest disturbance upsets it and then the voltages no longer exactly cancel and the uncancelled part appears as a small electrical signal in the receive coil. ('Signal' in electronics just means any small voltage or current you may wish to detect.)

If a target object comes in range of balanced coils it upsets the balance and so reveals its presence. This is the basic principle of what is known in Britain as the induction balance detector; in the United States it is called a transmit-receive or TR detector.

Beat Frequency Oscillator (BFO)

In the early days of radio, when receivers were not very sensitive or selective, they were provided with what was called a 'reaction' control. This produced a great improvement but needed very careful adjustment. If turned up too far it could produce an ear-splitting howl, not only from your own receiver but from your neighbour's as well. Your set was oscillating. To be precise it was oscillating and also slightly off tune; when exactly in tune with the incoming station, the howl or whistle disappeared. As you tuned in more and more closely the pitch of the note of the whistle dropped, getting lower and lower and finally vanishing.

The beat-frequency oscillator metal detector makes use of this oscillation. Its search coil is the tuning coil of a 'transmitter', and the transmission is tuned in rather like one of those early radios, only in this case the whistle is wanted. It is the user's means of keeping an ear to the search coil, so to speak. When a target comes into view its effect is to upset the

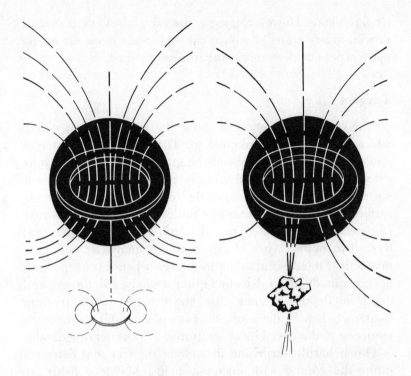

Fig 3   The electronic field of a BFO detector (*left*) weakened by the
presence of a conductive material and (*right*) concentrated by
the presence of a poor conductor

tuning, which is heard as a change in the pitch of the whistle
(Fig 3).

In terms of the amount of circuity required, the BFO
detector can be very modest and therefore relatively cheap—
from £16 to £40. It does however depend for its operation on
the user's sense of pitch, so is not for the tone deaf! It is ideal
for the younger members of the family and the beginner not
wishing to lay out too much at first. It has limited performance;
depth penetration is normally six inches on an object the size
of an old English penny. Because cheap components are used,
it is prone to be electrically unstable and be biased towards

ferrous metals. However, if used correctly, a BFO detector can provide many hours of enjoyment and locate items missed by more expensive detectors being incorrectly used.

Targets

So far we have been vague about the kind of target object which metal detectors respond to. There are all sizes, shapes and compositions of objects in the ground and naturally your detector will not respond equally to all of them. Common sense tells you that the bigger the object and the nearer the surface it is, the easier it will be to detect. But is silver as easy to detect as brass, or copper as iron? There are in practical terms two main classes of target object: magnetic and non-magnetic. Objects containing iron, even when it is in the form of rust, usually affect detectors quite strongly, size for size and depth for depth—in some cases too strongly for the treasure hunter's liking. PI detectors, for example, exhibit a distressing tendency to discover bits of scrap iron at considerable depths.

This is hardly surprising in view of the fact that detectors probe the ground with magnetic fields. Magnetic fields are inherent in magnetic materials such as iron. However, there are many materials, such as some kinds of iron ore, which have similar effects. For this reason some detector manufacturers classify small bits of scrap iron and iron ore by the same term— mineral—whether they are mineral in the technical mining sense or not.

Non-magnetic targets include all the common metals used in coin-making. Non-metallic substances such as carbon also conduct current and you may find that your detector responds to lumps of coke. It would be nice to think that diamonds, which are also a form of carbon, could be detected, but unfortunately diamond is non-conducting. If you find a diamond ring it will be the gold or silver you detect, not the stone.

The shape and size of a target object are crucial. A coin edge-on to the search coil is much harder to detect than the same coin broadside on. The reason is that in the broadside-on position current can flow easily in circular paths right round the rim of the coin. In the edge-on position current can flow only in little loops within the thickness of the coin. In general the bigger the current path, the easier an object is to detect. With some types of detector long thin objects like nails produce a response which varies according to the way the search coil passes over them. By making a second pass, at right angles to the first, you can often tell the shape of the object from the difference in response.

Discrimination

Ideally, a detector should tell the user everything he wants to know about the targets it detects—size, shape, composition, depth—the lot. In particular, detector owners would like to avoid spending time digging up junk such as silver paper, scrap iron, bottle caps and old tin cans. In recent years detectors have appeared on the market which are able, to a certain extent, to discriminate between targets.

The first and easiest discrimination to make is between ferrous (iron-containing) and non-ferrous metal. Even the humblest BFO detector usually possesses this ability to a limited extent, but how limited you soon realise after digging up a few dozen tin cans which, being made of mild steel, are ferrous and should be distinguishable from non-ferrous objects. Unfortunately they are both ferrous and conducting and the conducting effect fights the magnetic effect. It usually wins and makes the tin look like a non-ferrous object. This deception is aided by the thin layer of actual tin with which it is covered. Tin is non-ferrous. Most BFO detectors operate at a relatively high frequency (about 100 kilohertz, corresponding to a wavelength of about 3000 metres). At this sort of frequency currents flow mostly on the surface of an object and, since the surface of tinplate is non-ferrous, they tend to see only tin and not the underlying steel.

39

The answer is to use a low frequency so as to penetrate deeper into the object. When this is done, other types of discrimination become possible. Silver paper is aluminium foil and therefore non-ferrous, but being thin currents cannot penetrate deeply into it. So to a low-frequency detector silver paper looks different from thicker non-ferrous metal of similar size and shape. For technical reasons it is easier to incorporate a wide range of discrimination into IB and BFO detectors than PIs. PIs are inherently less sensitive to thin materials like silver paper than thick objects, but it is less easy to use them to distinguish between ferrous and non-ferrous objects. With the other kinds of detector both sorts of distinction can be made— always provided, of course, that your particular detector is designed to make them.

IB detectors can often be set so that they respond to ferrous targets by lapsing into silence; that is, they just ignore iron. That is one sort of positive discrimination. BFO discriminators may give a rise in pitch for non-ferrous and a fall for ferrous targets. Some detectors have a meter which makes the distinction by moving its pointer one way for ferrous and the other way for non-ferrous, and so on. Other forms of discrimination call for more skill on the part of the user. For example, some detectors respond to tinplate as non-ferrous when it is under the search head but as ferrous when it is just to one side. The user has to learn to interpret the response.

The purity of the metal in the target can have a great effect on discrimination. In general, pure metals are much better conductors of electricity than alloys. Consequently a modern British 'bronze' coin, which is fairly pure copper, may be much easier to distinguish from junk than a Roman bronze coin which is far from pure copper. Similarly pure gold may be a lot easier to distinguish than low-carat gold. These facts place a limit on the degree of discrimination which can be used in practice. Some discriminator detectors can be set in such a way that they accept British copper coins but reject modern 'silver' which is a copper-nickel alloy. For this reason some detector designers restrict the degree of discrimination to avoid rejecting cupro-nickel. The price you pay for this is their inability to reject some kinds of junk such as the thick aluminium kitchen foil used for cake cups and milk bottle caps.

A particularly intractable problem is posed by the ring-pulls from drink cans. These are made of fairly pure aluminium which is a good conductor and consequently they cannot be distinguished from rings and coins of other materials such as many grades of gold and silver! The end of the can which embodies the ring-pull is also aluminium and may produce a non-ferrous response even though the rest of the can is steel. The soft drinks and beer makers have a lot to answer for!

Ground Effects

You may think that the ground itself, being non-metallic, should have no effect on a detector, but harsh experience proves otherwise. Why? One reason is simply that there is a lot of ground and some of it is much closer to the search coil than are buried objects. Small amounts of conduction of the soil can for this reason have a large effect. Pure water is an electrical insulator but water with something dissolved in it can be a mild conductor. Soil water always has things dissolved in it and sea water is of course salty. So wet soil or sand as seen by a detector is always a mild conductor and as such a potential source of trouble. It produces spurious responses. PI detectors are inherently insensitive to the conductivity of the ground because the ground currents die away very quickly. BFO and IB detectors are inherently sensitive to ground effects but can be made insensitive by special circuit tricks. A detector with the facility of 'ground elimination balance' should be capable of being adjusted in such a way that it is unresponsive to the ground irrespective of whether the search head is high above the ground or close to it. Not all detectors for which the ground elimination balance facility is claimed can really be set to ignore all types of ground. They may work on the common but fail on the seashore.

If your detector does not have this facility (which can be an expensive extra) the best you can do is to set the balance while holding the head at its normal height (usually an inch above the surface). Movement of the head over the surface upsets the balance but you can learn to distinguish between the slowish changes of sound due to the ground and the quicker ones due to targets. As the detector passes from one type of soil to another (wetter to drier, for example) the instrument has to be reset. This nuisance is mitigated on some detectors by providing them with a button which, when pressed, instantly resets the balance for you. This relatively inexpensive improvement can transform an ordinary IB detector into one which is a delight to use over patchy ground, instead of a source of frustration.

One kind of ground effect which is a problem on some sites is a magnetic effect caused by particles of iron ore in the soil. It is not usually possible to balance this out on ground-effect-balance instruments, and even PI machines can be seriously affected. At least you know, when it hits you, that you are probably no worse off than the last treasure hunter who tried that site.

Two other kinds of ground effect are worth mentioning. One is ground or earth capacitance which afflicts some BFO detectors and causes a change in indication whenever the search head is brought near the ground, whatever the type of ground. The text-book cure is to equip the search coil with a Faraday screen or shield but this can hardly be done except by the manufacturer. It does *not* follow that any detector which is without a Faraday screen suffers from this effect: there are other ways of getting over it and in general they are better than using the screen. No decent detector should exhibit this effect.

The final ground effect is beneficial. As they lie in the ground and slowly corrode, metal objects cause the conductivity of the soil near them to increase. These 'haloes' of conducting soil make the object seem larger than it is to some detectors and therefore easier to find. Nature is not completely hostile.

Performance Criteria

As yet there is no agreed standard way of specifying the performance of a metal detector. In addition it should always be remembered that the performance of a detector in practice depends on the user as well as the instrument.

Sensitivity is often quoted as the depth at which a particular coin can be detected, assuming that the coin is flat-on to the head and that the soil has no ill effect on performance. Neither assumption is applicable to real coins on real sites. In general

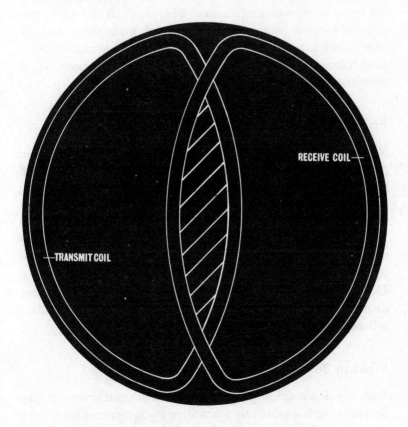

RECEIVE COIL—

—TRANSMIT COIL

Fig 4 The coil arrangement of an IB wide scan head detector; the shaded section represents the area of highest sensitivity

the very best detectors are capable of revealing a large coin at a depth of about a foot. It is unlikely that this limit will be improved upon very much because when the target is so far away even tiny amounts of ground effect become serious.

The effective area of the search head is always less than its actual area. In some old IB instruments it is very much less but most modern ones use a so-called wide scan head which should be effective across nearly the full width (Fig 4). Large heads are generally more sensitive than small ones, but make it difficult to pin-point small objects. A good compromise diameter is about eight inches. BFO and IB detectors are affected by changes in temperature which make them drift off tune or off balance. To minimise this some have auto-tune or auto-balance arrangements. Passing over a large close target may knock the detector off balance temporarily.

Frequency

While the frequency a detector operates on influences the performance, legally operation is determined by the Home Office. In order to minimise the risk of causing interference with the telecommunications services, metal detectors are permitted to operate only on frequencies between 16 and 150Khz. The laws in America are slightly different and relate to the electrical power output of the detector. Certain American BFO units operate on frequencies which are illegal in the United Kingdom and it is best to seek the advice of your local dealer before purchasing since a metal detector user requires a licence (see p 130).

What to Buy?

Basically, it should be the right detector *for you*: one user may do better with a relatively insensitive instrument which is very easy to use than a superb one which is 'hard to drive'. Get to know your own capabilities and choose your detector accordingly. And remember that while in general you get what you pay for, it is worth shopping around with the help of review articles in magazines or consumer advice publications.

Purchase your detector from a shop which specialises in treasure hunting equipment. Some suppliers will offer models on short trial periods, others will hire them out. Now and again you will find club organisations holding treasure hunting competitions and such occasions provide an excellent opportunity to have a chat, when the proceedings are over, and to actually see different models in service. Do remember, however, that technique is extremely important in hunting success and it is hardly fair for the beginner to pass snap judgements on the effectiveness, or otherwise, of any given model. Carry out tests and trials in your garden on a set of deliberate plants (sorry!) and compare the performance of different models.

Eventually you will finish up with the right model for its purpose and in the price range you can afford. Persevere and please remember that, whilst luck undoubtedly comes into it, success is a combination of going about things in the right way and patience. Research your site, learn to use your detector properly and results will come.

3 Searching Techniques and Equipment

Having successfully chosen the right type and model of detector, the next step is to learn how to use it in the most efficient and rewarding manner. Correct and intelligent use of one's equipment is essential if any success is to be achieved in searching; expensive and sophisticated equipment does not mean a thing if sound methods of operation are not used. Training oneself in good operational techniques is just as easy as getting into bad habits. As you are starting from scratch, why not start off the right way? It is the most natural thing in the world to want to rush off and try out your new-found gadget, but at least try to start off on the right foot, it will pay dividends later—perhaps sooner!

Before we start on sweeping techniques and patterns, let us study the machine itself and, in particular, the maker's instructions and recommendations and ensure that the correct battery is fitted.

The first thing of importance is to check that the detector is adjusted correctly to suit the height of the operator. Stand erect, arm dropped to the side, and adjust the machine so that the search head just lightly rests on the ground. If the machine is well designed it should have a nicely balanced feel. Do not swing the head from side to side raising it each end, but keep it level and parallel to the surface at all times (see Fig 5). It is very easy to miss finds if this simple and basic rule is not observed from the start. Do not try to cover too much ground too quickly. If you are provided with earphones, then do use them. They are essential in achieving that nth degree of sensitivity and delicacy in operation, and are worth buying

46

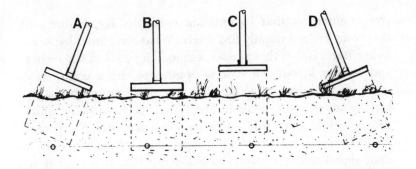

Fig 5   B indicates the correct positioning of the detector for maximum
effect; A, C and D show how a coin can be missed by poor use
of the detector even though it is within its range

as an extra. Interpreting the slight difference in audio and tone
level is largely a matter of experience and of knowing the
characteristics of one's particular piece of equipment and its
reactions to various kinds of objects. It is well worth doing
trials in one's own garden by deliberately burying pieces of
different size and type and at differing depths. Carefully note
the audio tone and meter reactions and learn to recognise
them. How simple or elaborate you care to make such home
trials is a personal matter and you can have quite a bit of fun
and, above all, learn a great deal about your equipment. This
will particularly be so if you have set up some trickier situations
such as planting pieces underneath each other, ie a larger
piece masking a smaller and more valueable find underneath it
and so on. By training your ear in this way you will recognise
real situations more quickly.

Wearing earphones out in the field on a hot day can be
tedious at times and you may well be tempted to wear them
round your neck but, if you do, then how can you possibly
hear that small faint signal which might well be the 'big find'?
Dedication is needed—it is all part and parcel of the thoroughness necessary to achieve success. Your equipment is doing
what it is designed to do, sending you information. It is up to

47

you to interpret that information correctly. Remember too that coins are not usually lost singly. What sometimes happens to beginners is that they receive a signal, dig down a few inches and retrieve a coin. They do not bother to check again; they cover up the spot and go on their way rejoicing but probably leaving many more behind. The signal, perhaps being quite strong, would have told an experienced operator a different story. Coins which are deposited on their edges give only a faint signal and are easily passed over. This is why it is so essential to develop the art of listening to and interpreting signals to as high a science as possible. Paul Stokes of Plymouth read the signals he receives from his own particular detector as follows:

1. Silver paper, coke: Faint buzzing, increasing in intensity, reading maximum output directly over the object, then decreasing conversely. The buzzing sound is exactly the same type as heard when tuning the detector.

2. Metal can pull-rings, tin cans: Signal has a slight sharpness to its edge but the buzzing has a metallic hollow ring about it, very slight but noticeable, almost a tinny sound.

3. Brass, copper, cupro-nickel, silver: Sharp signal, no increase or decrease, buzzing has a sweeter tone than 2, more solid sounding yet a softness.

4. Gold: Sharp signal, as with 3, buzzing has a clarity of its own, a ring to its tone, solid sounding yet jarringly acute, almost as though screaming.

5. Iron, steel, etc.: Signal sharp but slightly fuzzy at the edge, buzzing has a coarseness to it.

People 'hear' sounds differently, but in the early stages the sounds described above may be a useful guide.

Always remember to tune in your detector before starting to sweep. It is advisable to obtain a faint signal as this avoids the possibility of the signal drifting further towards the null, thereby reducing the detection range. Having a small amount of sound also tells you that your machine is operational. Learn too to carry your detector in one hand and dig with the other.

48

This will take a little mastering but it is a great time-saver as you can establish whether the object you have located is still in the earth or in the plug you have partially extracted.

Now the word digging has cropped up it is as well to clear up some misunderstandings that exist in so many beginners' minds and, regrettably, in the minds of some who should know better. Beginners often imagine that somehow a lot of sheer hard deep digging, using a good old-fashioned spade, is and must be an essential part of treasure hunting. Nothing could be further from the truth! There will be the odd exception, of course, and more so perhaps now that recent models are giving much deeper penetration. It is a fact, however, that most finds have been made only a few inches under the surface and that the tool most favoured by some of our best known hunters is a long-handled screwdriver, ice pick or anything similar such as an old knife-sharpening steel.

Treasure hunters should never leave any signs behind of their visit to a site. Having pinpointed your find by maximum signal strength and keeping your detector steady in one hand, insert your long-handled screwdriver, trowel or similar tool in front of the spot at an angle of about forty-five degrees and push forward cutting a slit in the ground. Bring the shaft back and go forward again and cut a further slit at an angle in the form of a V. It will then be possible to lever out the plug of earth so obtained on a hinge and your detector should be able to tell you where your find is. Alternatively, cut threequarters of a circle round the find with a trowel (see illustration), fold the turf back and extract the find. Having recovered successfully, and also having rechecked that there is nothing further there, carefully replace any loose soil and the plug of earth and gently tread it back again. These methods should cause a minimum of damage to grass and leave the site looking like it was, more or less, when you started operations. If anything more drastic is required in the way of recovery, do all you can to minimise disturbance and restore the ground properly. Avoid digging round young trees as damage to their roots will

One method of extracting a find

cause them to die; in any case, it is most unlikely that anything will be buried there. When digging round trees, replace all soil carefully and tread it down thoroughly to avoid damage.

Special trowels can be bought from your dealer. There is a school of thought which deprecates the screwdriver method because of the risk of scratching and damaging finds. You do not need, nor indeed is it desirable, to use a new screwdriver which in any case could be expensive. Find something which is quite blunt and smooth. A cheap trowel with a rivetted handle is a false economy as a strongly made one will last years.

Choosing a suitable type of site and the necessary researching are covered in Chapters 4, 5 and 6. At this stage, therefore, we will simply deal with the technique of sweeping, hunting and searching. Thoroughness is the key word to success here as the words hunting and searching imply. Whilst your quarry is not likely to run away there is, nevertheless, a very good chance that you will miss it if your sweeps are carried out in a perfunctory and haphazard way. Ordinarily one should make a thorough search of a small area and make return visits as necessary but you may be short of time and of opportunity to revisit the site you are searching. If this is the case, you must employ the most effective alternative—the criss-cross search pattern (Fig 6). This entails dividing the area into large convenient squares by hunting along the left-hand perimeter in a straight line, then moving twenty feet at a time towards the right-hand perimeter searching in parallel lines to the first. When the right-hand perimeter is reached, the process is repeated but at right angles to the first rows. During these sweeps, any finds should be marked and returned to when the criss-cross pattern is completed. It is often the case that when one find is made, others will be found close by, particularly in the case of coins. A more thorough and detailed search can be undertaken by then marking out an area approximately ten feet square around each find and dividing this into convenient strips that can be swept comfortably (Fig 7). This is a compromise system of hunting to use only when time and circumstances are against you. Now to return to the thoroughness referred to earlier.

It is a good idea, and sound practice too, to wear a belt

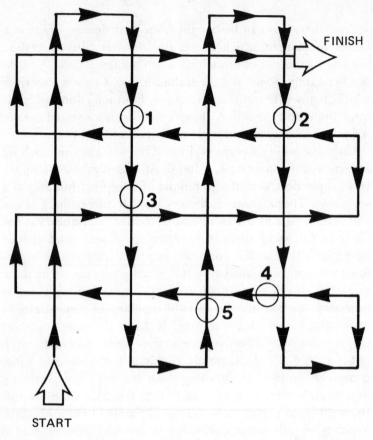

FINISH

START

Fig 6   The criss-cross search pattern

looped through two pouches or bags—one to put finds in, one for rubbish. These can be made of denim or sailcloth. Wear comfortable, good quality 'gardening' gloves or industrial weight plastic or rubber gloves. Never throw back, or discard dug-up junk. Collect it together and dispose of it systematically —otherwise you yourself may finish up with it again next time around.

The best technique to use in an open area is to clearly define and then mark out, with pegs and twine, the parcel of land to be searched, dividing it into manageable strips, comfortably with-

52

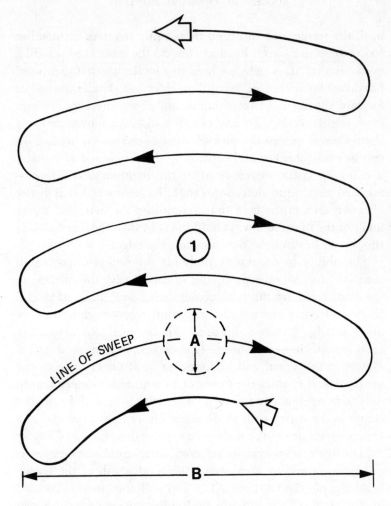

Fig 7　Concentrated search pattern
　　　A = width of detector's pick-up area
　　　B = length of a comfortable sweep

in your reach. To achieve maximum searching efficiency, remember to keep the search head parallel to the ground, particularly at the end of the sweep. This is best achieved by moving the arm and not the body. When the first lane has been swept, just carry on with the one next to it, and so on, until the whole area has been thoroughly covered. Remember too to keep the search head as close to the ground as possible, even 'ironing' it. A detector held two inches above the ground has lost two inches of ground penetration. Each movement forward during the sweep should not allow any gaps, so aim for a slight overlap. In any case the distance moved forward should never exceed the pick-up area of the search head. This can be easily checked and verified by the simple test of moving a coin across the search head at the manufacturer's recommended maximum detection range. Remember that it is the effective area of the coin that determines the detection range and not the mass, so always hold the coin with the face towards the search head of the detector, not the edge.

The ability to accurately pinpoint the find is important if time is not to be wasted digging unnecessarily; the method to use is dictated by the type of detector being used. BFO and single-coil types are usually true total response detectors. In other words, their pick-up area can be measured across the total area of the search head. This makes pinpointing difficult. However, the signal will be found to be stronger towards the centre which enables the operator to detune his detector until only a faint signal is received, when the find will be in the centre of the search coil. IB detectors either have a circular coil arrangement or are the wide scan type as described in Chapter 2. The wide scan type is referred to as total response as it produces a pick-up area across the total width of the search head and not the total area. The find will, therefore, be located on the central line. When a find is located, the operator can memorise the position of the line and then rotate the head through ninety degrees and sweep along this line until he locates the find in the centre of the search head. Circular coil arrangements are usually larger than the diametrical type but have a smaller receive coil situated in the centre of the search head. This has the effect of reducing the pick-up area to the small central circle. It therefore allows for quite accurate pinpointing without any additional sweeping. Understanding the characteristics of your particular detector will greatly assist you in your searching and recovery procedures.

Grassy pathways through woodlands, bridlepaths, old public rights of way, etc, can often be a lucrative source of finds. To go over them in a cursory manner is a waste of time and effort as they require very thorough searching in a methodical way.

As the reader will have seen in Chapter 1, some of the most spectacular finds have been the result of research, sometimes extending back over three years or more. Such research, often carried out with the help of the local library, can be particularly fascinating in discovering the history of one's own locality. Often it becomes serious detective work resulting in a build-up of information which might lead to a successful hunch paying off. The obvious often escapes notice but it is a recognised fact that some sites will be more likely to bear fruit than others. Wherever people have congregated, and for the longer the period the better, then the bigger the chance there must be of retrieving relics. If the site is one with connections going back over centuries, say an ancient bridlepath such as the Pilgrims Way in Kent, or a Roman road, then the chances of really worthwhile finds are much greater.

Check List of Useful Equipment

Carrying bag

Ordnance Survey map of locality

Compass

Torch

Spare batteries

Polythene bags for finds

Pegs and line

Rubber or industrial gloves

Notebook and pencil

Belt with carrying pouches

Tidetables (if appropriate)

Warm waterproof clothing (Ex-Government surplus stores are good source)

Boots/Strong shoes

(Additional equipment for river and beach work is listed on page 78)

4 Inland Sites

An inland site could theoretically extend from Lands End to John o' Groats and equally breadthwise across the country, so there is plenty of scope! Rivers and lakes are covered along with other watery sites in the next chapter. No matter in which direction you look, there is a chance that there is something hidden away just waiting to be dug up or dislodged. Because of the pattern of human behaviour over the centuries, however, some localities will prove a much more lucrative source of finds than others. In the main people are gregarious creatures, so we are looking for any places where human activity of some kind or another has taken place. Researching, or just plain thinking about what kind of activity this might have been, will provide all the necessary clues and incentive. Let us therefore start to consider the possibilities, for whilst you might be fortunate enough to turn something up anywhere, the chances of success are much greater if the project is approached on a sound basis of deduction and logic.

Basically, the greater the number of people who have gathered in one place, the greater the number of items which will have been lost or hidden. Apart from obvious places like village greens and commons, search out shelving hollows where spectators could have watched prize fights, cock fights, dog racing and gaming. Such activities, being slightly outside the law, could have been broken up precipitately with the strong chance of stake money being abandoned in the rush. In the 1920s when unemployment was high, men used to play pitch and toss, often losing the whole of their week's dole money in one day. The police tried to break up these games, and as a result the players would scatter and many coins would be left in the dust or grass.

Fairgrounds

Fairgrounds have always provided the coin hunter with a lot of fun and a good return for a few hours' work. When the word fairground is mentioned most people will immediately think of dodgemcars, cakewalks, coconut shies and all the trappings of the modern catch-penny type of operation. However, the actual fairground itself may, by ancient right, charter or tradition, be centuries old. Some village charters go back to the twelfth and thirteenth centuries and specific days such as saint's days were allotted, perhaps twice a year, for a fair to be held there.

Careful research into old maps, parish records and old books can reveal the sites of horse fairs, hiring fairs, goose fairs, frost

A fair in London's East End, 1912; many coins would be lost in the bustle and excitement (*Radio Times Hulton Picture Library*)

fairs and many others. Older local people can often direct you to traditional sites. Place names can provide good clues, but remember that many different spellings of the same place can be expected. It could be rewarding to trace the routes leading to livestock fairs as well as the drove roads used for centuries; places where two or more of these meet could be a fruitful searching area, as could obvious overnight stopping places. But be prepared for disappointments; months of research tracing a site gleaned from snippets of information here and there can lead you to the exact location, now beautifully preserved under a recent housing development.

Remember, however, that if the fairground is on a village green, then it is almost certainly where the other village activities take place. Cricket, for example, and digging holes in cricket pitches is not recommended! Village greens are objects of special affection. You must seek and obtain permission from the clerk to the local parish council before proceeding. If the site is really old, then all kinds of small finds can turn up quite apart from medieval coins, such as semi-precious shoe buckles which were often silver.

The modern fairground will offer very quick rewards if you can cover and search the site almost immediately after the operators have moved off. An old treasure hunter who has followed the hobby since the very early days claims to have picked up over six hundred coins in five hours in such circumstances. These will, of course, be modern coins mostly but do check each one for date; some are worth much more than face value. Old threepenny pieces too are worth finding. The experienced prospector will quickly know where to start searching—many clues will indicate the position of stalls etc. When the stalls have just been moved, it is an easy matter to identify such areas as the grass is well trodden down. However, even if it is some weeks or months afterwards it is still possible to see where they were as the grass tends to grow differently in these particular areas. Quite apart from coinage there are the usual small items of jewellery—rings and so forth—to be found.

As with all sites, plan well ahead, get up early and give yourself plenty of time so that you can work slowly and methodically. There could be perhaps as many as two hundred and fifty detectable coins in the area you have mapped out. If you try and cover it in an hour the chances are you will finish up missing most of them. By giving yourself ample time you will probably locate most of them.

Footpaths

Footpaths offer much scope for study and have yielded some good finds, but again there is a great deal more to it than appears at first sight. A study of ley lines may help in searching for the routes of ancient trackways. The theory is that sites of ancient importance align. Using an Ordnance Survey map, plot stone circles, standing stones, barrows, tumuli, mottes and baileys, hillforts, earthworks, churches, abbeys and other traditionally sacred or ancient features. You will frequently find three-, four- and five-point groups of alignment, or even more. The countryside is a web of old paths and rights of way, usually plainly marked by signposts. Ordnance Survey maps will quickly show some of the thousands of miles of ancient tracks and paths that criss-cross our island. It is worth researching back further than these maps which only go back to the early eighteen hundreds, although they omit little as a rule. Footpaths are usually fairly productive and encouraging to the beginner and it is not often that the prospector will come home without something to show unless he is unfortunate enough to choose a path that has recently been well worked over. Books on local history or glossy county and country magazines are usually informative. The sort of information, for example, that one might be able to glean is where the highwaymen used to haunt, quite apart from other useful snippets of purely local interest. But cross-check information where possible—a treasure hunter has on occasion proved local history books wrong by charting and plotting finds and dating them. False clues and wrong information and captions can appear in newspapers and other publications. The Public Records Office tends to be reliable since facts are recorded at the time for posterity. Some paths have become re-routed over the years by farmers, others obliterated by circumstances such as forest fires or have become so overgrown and disused as to have become forgotten. Some were really roads in medieval times and carried coaches or carts. An excellent book of the subject is *No Through Road*.

As a general rule those paths which are only, say, three feet in width do not yield too well. The type of track or path which was once a road and a positive route of communications is a far better bet. Quite apart from the wheeled transport that used them, the labourer would perhaps trudge them twice a day to his place of work, or the pilgrim on his pilgrimage, knights and nobles, kings and beggars, on foot, on horseback or by coach, many of them carrying valuables, some to be set upon by robbers and others to hide their valuables before entering the village to spend the night. Such tracks became very rutted and muddy and the pedestrian would, therefore, tend to skirt around the edge. It is something we all do. Where finds have been made they quite often have materialised not merely two or three feet from the edge of the track, but as much as ten yards away because of the traveller's need to get out of the mud and the ruts. Old paths and tracks tend to get overgrown, so a winter visit when all the nettles and the like have died away will make searching a lot easier.

Research may prove that some very old houses were in fact inns centuries ago and therefore paths leading to and from them will have been used by travellers and wayfarers. In the remoter areas paths and tracks leading from farms to villages and market towns are often very old. They were certainly a means of communication, taking goods to market, farm workers going about their work or perhaps to visit the local tavern. As a rule paths which are under fifty years old are not worth the work and worry. The older the better is the maxim to follow, particularly those dating back to Roman times.

The typical plug of compacted grass and mud which forms above a
a buried coin

Many of the older tracks such as the Pennine Way kept to
high ground for reasons of safety. The traveller could more
easily keep a weather-eye open for hostile tribes or others who
might wish to waylay or ambush him and relieve him of his
valuables. Being so old, one might expect a wide chronological
range of finds but, unless you are very lucky, you will need to
persevere. The most productive parts of our older track and
byway system would be fords or likely sheltering places—anywhere which would appear to have been a possible resting place
in fact. Sometimes a chat to the locals will elicit useful information as to finds made in the past indicating that a further
search of the particular area might be fruitful. When finds are
made along these old traditional tracks, they usually prove to
be worth the effort.

To return to the more commonplace footpath—through
woods, across commons or village greens—there are several
factors which are common to all. Having been well trodden,
the surface tends to be compacted and therefore objects which
have been dropped and walked over sink much more slowly
than in loose soil and remain fairly near to the top, within a

61

few inches of the surface—sometimes only two or three inhces down. Another reason for this is that the effects of the weather tend to wash or blow the surface away or the passage of feet can wear it down. Even a detector with moderate performance such as a cheaper BFO will get results in these circumstances. Sometimes it may be noticeable that paths leading from out-lying areas to various parts of a village will meet in one particular area as they get towards their objective; this might be the church or village hall or inn. As obviously this last section will have been the most used, it should prove the most fruitful to search.

When searching footpaths through forests and wood, re-member that any large clearing could have been the site of a now-demolished house or cottage. However, don't forget that all footpaths belong to someone—an individual, a body or a local authority—and permission must always be obtained to search. Remember too that it is particularly important to fill in holes thoroughly and for the soil to be well tamped down. Sprained ankles or worse caused by thoughtless detector users will do nothing for the hobby's public image.

Sheila and Bert Freeman made an exciting find when searching a footpath which ran through woods at a slight incline. They found what at first sight appeared to be a badly damaged blazer button, but on closer examination was found to to be a gold Gallo-Belgic stater. Further sweeps produced more and, the following day, a further nine; the Freemans then bought a discriminator model of detector which gave greater depth penetration and eliminated the problems of ground effect. More searching brought the total to twenty-three staters. They were later approached by the local arch-aeological society who asked for details of the location of the find; the Freemans not only took them to the site but assisted in a meticulous excavation which resulted in the discovery of a further twenty-seven staters. The original twenty-three staters have been declared treasure trove and have been valued at more than £15,000.

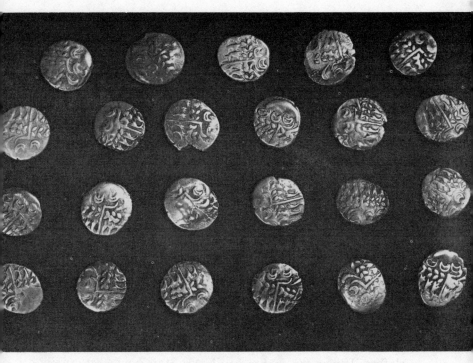

Sheila and Bert Freeman's magnificent find of twenty-three gold Gallo-Belgic staters

Public Parks

Public parks are not very good for single finds of any great significance. Where there is, or has been, a bandstand there is reasonable encouragement for coin hunters. Bandstands were quite an institution in grandfather's day and there could well be worthwhile finds of Victorian coins and other small objects. Remember too that there was often a large ring of deckchairs, which are notorious for emptying trouser pockets, extending back many yards all round the bandstand.

Parkland

Parklands such as those that surround our large stately homes are not usually worth searching although there is the outside chance of a hoard turning up if the house is old. Bearing in mind the vast acreage involved, however, it would be rather like looking for the proverbial needle in a haystack. Another rather fruitless activity is searching the average village pond which, as a rule, only yields up rubbish. The drought of 1976 revealed the contents of most in stark detail. The sort of place that does prove encouraging in a small way, however, is a country bus shelter or stopping place.

The early Victorians loved their picnics. They were not blessed or cursed, whichever your viewpoint, with the 'horse-less carriage' and were not in consequence as lazy as the modern picnicker who, if he cannot settle down with his status symbol a maximum of ten feet away, will not stop. The Victorians were prepared to walk or cycle miles to a popular beauty spot and there to settle down to their potted meat, shrimps, winkles and cucumber sandwiches. Suitably refreshed they would indulge in family sports; how easy it must have been for them to lose odd personal items from their voluminous clothes. If you can manage to locate these places, there is a good chance of Victoriana turning up. Again, a chat in the local with the older inhabitants will often produce the necessary nostalgia and the information you seek.

Battlefields

Battlefields are well documented and often clearly defined and marked on maps; the research already completed for anyone to read in the local liberary or museum. However, reference libraries are like the Public Records Office or town hall—to do your research means spending hours there, making sketches and copious notes and it can be difficult to find the necessary time. Old fields of battle are usually under the protection of the Ancient Monuments Act and, in this respect, are categorised very much in the same way as archaeological sites. Do be very sure you are on safe ground, in more ways than one, before searching old battlefields. You can be quite severely dealt with if caught and either imprisoned or, at least, very heavily fined and your equipment confiscated too. Tracing the routes of military roads, especially in Scotland, is also rewarding.

Farmland

Farmland holds many possibilities, but clearly the first thing is to get specific permission to search and to take every care not to damage crops. Farmers are much more likely to give permission in the autumn after crops have been harvested; in the winter the vegetation dies down and the frosts break up the ground, making things easier for the metal detector user. Mr Mayes of Thetford in Norfolk was searching farmland on a bitterly cold April day in 1975. Prior to leaving for home, he went to collect his headphones which he had left on the ground, but still had his detector tuned. He received a signal a yard across where the headphones lay but, as it had started to snow, he had to wait— with ill-concealed impatience—for the next evening. He again asked the farmer's permission in view of the size of the object, and the farmer's son and Mr Mayes, armed with a shovel, went to investigate. Eighteen inches below the surface they uncovered a large bronze cauldron eighteen inches across, inside

The collection of Roman bronze cauldrons found by Mr Mayes in Norfolk farmland

which were carefully packed two small bronze cauldrons, two bronze bowls, two bronze fruit dishes and yet another flat dish. The chains on which the large cauldron had hung were beside it, all of Roman origin dating back to AD350–400.

Mary Aaron, with her husband and sons, farms Fryston Hall Farm near Castleford in Yorkshire. Fryston Hall was used for billeting soldiers during the 1914–18 War but has now been demolished. Many famous people including Disraeli and Thomas Thackeray were guests of Lord Houghton there and Mary, who has access, has made a wide variety of finds in the area—army cap badges and buttons, a button bearing Lord Houghton's arms, a 1797 cartwheel penny, a George III penny, a thirteenth-century 'counter coin' from the city of Tours, Victorian copper and silver coins, an antique pistol, a cast-iron garden seat and a ring lost sixty years previously by an old lady living nearby who was absolutely overwhelmed by its return. She has learned to be curious about any odd objects on the farm—she spotted a piece of metal in the toolbox of her husband's tractor which had been turned up by ploughing. He used it to scrape mud from the ploughshare, but it turned out to be part of the blade of a druid sword of about 1500BC.

Buildings

Victorian and Edwardian buildings offer hundreds of potential hiding places for interesting items; older buildings are unlikely to be available for the treasure hunter for searching. Look under skirting boards especially near doors—a piece of wire bent into a hook will winkle out coins which have rolled there; look inside locks—coins were often put inside as a draught excluder. Search lofts, try chimney breasts, loose mantlepieces and fireplaces, floorboards, cellars. Remember that it used to be considered safer to hide valuables at home rather than entrusting them to the early banks. Outside, look round buttresses, under eaves, near wells—in fact any place of some significance which could be easily remembered by the hider.

Searching the floorboards of
a house undergoing
extensive alterations

Mines and Quarries

Provided that you take great care and heed any notices, old
mining areas can prove interesting hunting grounds. You may
find old company tokens, coins, picks and other tools, buckles,
bottles and lamps. Sand and gravel pits and quarries also
offer possibilities, and their sites can be traced on the one-inch
Ordnance Survey maps—again, place names will often give
useful clues. Disused pits and quarries often became used as
town and village tips.

Racecourses

Racecourses are a good source of finds and some of them date
back to the 1700s. By now, some of the older ones have disappeared altogether, but it is sometimes possible to see where

these were once situated from early Ordnance Survey maps. There is the site of an old course at Bridge, near Canterbury, for example. With the large amounts of money constantly changing hands between punters and bookies and, in the old days, by personal wagers, it would not be surprising to find relics such as snuff boxes of the period, rings, buckles and buttons as well as coins lying about. After a modern race meeting there should be a very good chance of finding cupro-nickel coins, rings and bracelets and all the usual items that detach themselves from their owners. Motor racing meetings are another possibility; crowds gather round the edge of the track in order to get a better view of impending disasters, particularly on hairpin bends and the start and finish areas.

So much of a successful aptitude for treasure hunting is really common sense, being a good detective and bothering to read anything which may prove useful in building up a picture of the past. Having done your homework on paper to the extent that you are convinced that it all adds up, the next thing is to go out into the field and practice your searching techniques thoroughly. Understand your equipment and ex-ploit its characteristics fully and you should start achieving success, but do not expect miracles at once. Richard Davies, whose opinion I respect, told me that the more he searches, the greater the proportion of older coins he turns up. This is not accidental, of course; it merely means that the more he dedicates himself, the more expert he becomes. The whole of our country-side is potentially one large site extending to all points of the compass. It is up to you to decide what project to follow up but do have a specific aim in view if you want to succeed, although of course you may be lucky and stumble on some-thing interesting accidentally.

5 Water Sites

Now to the water's edge, whether it be salt or fresh water, flowing or still. A new set of considerations involving a knowledge of the elements and their effect on the environment emerge at once. Generally speaking, unless disturbed by farming operations, building development, replanning, motorway building or such aids to modern living, earth remains undisturbed, unless eroded, for centuries. The same, however, cannot be said where water is concerned; the effect of storms on our coastline, the slow but decisive effect of silting in estuaries and rivers, draining of lakes and ponds, rerouting of rivers and streams and erosion of cliffs combine to give an ever-changing situation. The effect of tides should be understood, normally changing twice in the course of twenty-four hours as the pull of sun and moon make themselves felt. Canals too present a changing picture; some sections are drained, some restored, the water level in others allowed to drop.

Rivers

Let us look at rivers first, however. Since the early days of civilisation, man has been drawn inexorably to the river's edge. It has provided water for cooking, drinking, washing and for manufacturing purposes; it has proved a convenient means of transport both for peaceful and warlike purposes; it has been a territorial dividing line and a barrier. The majority of our major cities and towns are situated on rivers, often originating as early settlements. In effect, therefore, from time immemorial people have congregated around such places and left behind them a treasure trail to be followed by the keen prospector. Many coins and valuables must have been lost in the waters of rivers when paying a toll to a ferryman or perhaps transacting business. In the course of battle the river has often represented an obstacle and a barrier to a retreating army unable to effect a quick escape to the other side. Historical research quickly indicates such places and where it would be reasonable to suppose that armour and weaponry might well be found. Traditionally, the superstitious Romans always threw a coin into a river before crossing it, which makes searching a known Roman river crossing site a promising prospect. As with other aspects of treasure hunting, it is important to do your homework first.

Where do you look then? There are literally thousands of miles of riverside and canals in this country, though a great deal of it would probably prove to be non-productive because of the lack of human association. Examine and research the uses to which different stretches of waterway have been put over the centuries. Having carried out preliminary research in the local library or museum, a visit to an inn and a chat to the locals over a pint will sometimes provide useful colour. People love talking about the good old days and can provide constructive information although sometimes it has to be taken with that proverbial pinch of salt. Once again, old maps and reference books will show where traditional crossing places and old bridges were situated. It was not unknown for early bridges, being poorly constructed, to collapse and deposit the poor traveller and his possessions into the waters of the river below, and early bridges were sometimes without parapets. Even before the advent of bridges and wheeled traffic, merchants and travellers using packhorses would attempt to cross to the other side. Such crossings were fraught with difficulty and danger, and merchandise and valuables—not to mention lives—were occasionally lost. Old maps will show where stretches of river have been diverted, perhaps to reclaim land or to minimise flooding.

The sites of medieval wharves have provided many interesting finds including articles lost overboard by foreign seamen; whilst mostly what one might loosely describe as bric-a-brac, nevertheless articles such as badges, buttons and objects of no consequence at the time are now collectors' pieces. This applies also to industrial shipping wharves where a search at low tide often provides an interesting item or two. Many of our ancient ports such as Sandwich in Kent and Rye in Sussex are now a considerable distance from the sea as silting up has occurred over the centuries. Comparison between ancient and modern charts and maps will reveal the old landing places.

Places where the public go swimming are usually productive as, not surprisingly, large numbers of personal possessions—money, watches, etc—get lost while changing. Rings, too, have a habit of slipping off a bather's finger whilst swimming or playing at the water's edge as chilly water makes the finger contract. Coins are usually modern but quite a number of Victorian origin have been found.

When an object falls into a river it is pushed, pulled, dragged and rolled downstream. The weight and shape of the object, as well as the direction and strength of the current in relation to where it actually fell in, will determine its final resting place. The current will push the object to a position where there is no further force to propel it, and there it will rest on the river bed and gradually get covered if the bottom is muddy. Usually the first bend downstream of a ford, ferry, pub or village is the most productive. Remember, however, that it is always the inner part of the bend where the flow is quieter and slower. Observe the flow of a river on a bend carefully, take note of the differing speeds of the current on the outside of the sweep compared with the inside. The factors which will greatly influence conditions are the strength and speed of the current, the depth and volume of the water being moved, the shape

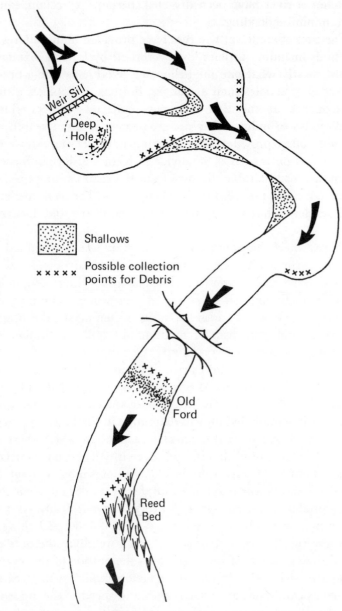

Fig 8   Typical positions for finds in rivers

and position of obstacles such as a landing stage or buildings, bridges or islands, the prevailing wind and, of course, the state of the tide if tidal (Fig 8). Obstacles which are at right angles to the main flow will tend to trap articles on the side facing the current. Finds will also be made, however, behind such obstacles, because when the main current rushes past the edges of the obstacle it tends to create a vacuum. The water then pushes in to fill this vacuum causing an eddy and sucking in small items from the main current. Generally speaking, eddies and whirlpools are created by obstructions and obstacles which are wider at the end facing the mainstream or current. These are known as hotspots. Lost articles will travel down the river in the main current until they reach a bend where they will be deposited on the inner bank. A silt shelf tends to build up at this spot and is well worth searching; sieving is a good method of locating finds. In these conditions, objects of a similar small size are often found together. Whilst advantageous in some respects, this also means that unwanted items such as rusty nails and other small iron objects tend to congregate as well. It is for this reason that, in such circumstances, a detector which can accurately pinpoint and is biassed towards non-ferrous metals is the best bet.

It is comparatively easy to calculate the characteristics of the main current by sketching a map of the river and plotting the speed and direction of floating items drifting past. It is then possible to imagine where coins or objects might have been dropped and lost, plotting their probable course and noting where the flow strength is weakest. You will see the pattern of currents and eddies best from a bridge or similar high point. Try wearing polarised sunglasses when peering into the water as these will cut down reflection.

The important thing to consider is the effect that the change of the tide will have on items on the river bed. Once the direction and characteristics of the ebbing current have been plotted, wait until the bottom of the tide and draw in the obstacles on your map. This will help you to see and determine the course of any underwater currents and turbulence that were not evident at high water. A hump in the river bed for example would cause water to rush over it and increase the strength of the flow at this point. It is worth remembering that the lowest tide is always two days after full moon. Tidetables are available from local shops or river authorities, and show tidal heights as well as times.

Having mapped out possible hotspots that appear to offer reasonable prospects, commence a search—but wrap up well with protective clothing and wellies or waders. Before searching, however, there are necessary precautions to be taken. Mud can be very deceptive and extremely treacherous. You can find yourself up to your waist in no time and, with no assistance within hail plus the absolute certainty of a rising tide, can be in a position of extreme danger. A handy rope secured to the bank, or a board or plank at hand is a wise precaution but, in any case, always probe in front of you with a stout stick before proceeding further. Make sure there is firm ground not too far below the mud. Tread warily! Do not go too far from some means of getting out and if in any doubt make sure you secure yourself with that rope or have that plank handy. It could save your life. Be constantly aware of the water's progress around you as the tide starts to turn and be sure to have an exit available.

If you want to spend the maximum time searching, start as soon as it is feasible with the tide dropping. You should then have four to five hours. Mark out the search area by sighting on natural objects such as rocks, trees or features of some kind— maybe a rusted bedstead! When you have reached the end of your search area, turn and hunt in the opposite direction along the water's edge. As the tide continues to drop you can continue to search systematically. Unless you have reasonably intimate local knowledge, it is not always easy to judge the rate of the tidal rise and fall or what area it is reasonable to

Underwater searching near an old river crossing

expect to cover. If your area is too long in relation to the rate of drop you will miss stretches of the river bed; conversely if it is too short you will be covering ground over again.

It is almost certain that when a productive site is found there will be a high proportion of iron present. One method of getting round this is to drag a fairly powerful magnet over the area. Due to their condition it is not always easy to identify finds at once, although their shape should be indicative. Learn to be conscious of shape rather than initial appearance—you will soon develop the necessary sixth sense and avoid discarding collectable items. The magnet does, of course, help to distinguish between the ferrous and non-ferrous.

It is important because of the wet conditions to employ the methods of detector handling outlined in Chapter 3. Hold the detector in one hand and dig with the other. Remember tidal water is salt and this very quickly attacks and corrodes metal. Avoid laying your detector down where it will get wet; sand and mud too are distinct enemies. Wrap the control box in a plastic bag secured with a rubber band. If, however, the control box does get wet, disconnect the batteries and flush the detector all over with fresh water and dry it with a fan or hair dryer. Then lubricate the control spindles, taking care to avoid excess oiling.

Club members and individual prospectors are a common sight now at low tide working on the foreshores of Old Father Thames from Teddington Lock, where the upper reaches become locked-in and non-tidal, down river through the Pool of London to the estuary. At low water, the exposed patches—often shingle in places and therefore firm and safe ground on which to search—have proved lucrative and productive areas for finds. The historical richness of London cannot help but provide the amateur treasure hunter with tremendous interest and reward. The tidal reaches come under the jurisdiction of the Port of London Authority from whom permission should be sought to search along the banks. During the exceptional summer and drought conditions of the summer of 1976, the river was at its lowest level for many years, particularly through Putney and Richmond. Richmond has what is known as a half-lock and when the lock at Teddington just above is closed, the water can be at an extremely low level and it is possible with a pair of waders to get out almost to the middle of the river to search. Roman coins are always turning up in various states of condition but antique weaponry as well as Celtic coins, brooches and relics of the Civil War have yielded themselves up to treasure hunters quite frequently, particularly in the Kew area.

Where bridges have been built in the last hundred years or so, many finds of the Victorian period have been made along the neighbouring foreshore. Between Southwark and Tower Bridge, relics of all periods have been discovered, the river banks around London Bridge being prolific in finds of the Roman era. When the existing Kew Bridge was constructed there was a most interesting discovery of an arsenal of Bronze and Iron Age weapons. The area where the River Wandle joins the Thames has yielded some very fine examples of ancient weaponry. During dredging operations in the nineteenth century, a most important Iron Age relic was brought up. Known as the Battersea Shield, it is now in the British Museum together with many of the other treasures found in the area. Indeed, all along the banks of the tidal Thomas there is an unending source of treasure and historical interest.

Whilst the Thames, with its background of changing civilisation and pageantry, holds pride of place, there are many such rivers all over the country where history has similarly been made. All are rewarding if intelligently researched, particularly so where there are old castles and where battles are known to have taken place. The northern town of Berwick, for example, changed hands more than a dozen times during the wars between the Scots and the English. Quite a few interesting relics from these troubled times have been found on the fore-shores of the Tweed, particularly at Halidon Hill. The Firth of Forth is known to be rewarding in the bridge area. On the

77

banks of the Tyne, too, there have been worthwhile finds of Roman origin, particularly along the foreshore at Newcastle which has also produced finds from all periods. Upnor Castle on the River Medway, and Rochester Castle just a little further upstream, were the scene of belligerent exchanges between the Dutch, who frequently marauded, and the defenders. The rivers of our eastern seaboard, facing Europe, have all seen their share of clamour and turmoil and provide much to challenge the treasure hunter.

In non-tidal waters there are differences in search technique. According to the need to maintain a desirable and reasonably constant level, the water authority will control the ebb by the use of weirs and sluices. The places to look for are the shallows where ferrying or fording has taken place. If the water is clear there will not be a problem, but beware of hidden holes; should the water be muddy, then probe ahead before moving. Fording places usually have a firm and shingly bed and are shallow or they would not have been so chosen of course. Always work upstream so that finds are not obscured by the mud churned up by your own boots.

Before piped water was widespread, water was collected from springs and wells and these provide another hunting ground if approached carefully. Brick or stone surrounds were often built around the springs because of the mud, and some were even covered over to keep leaves and twigs out. Victorian coins and artefacts are possible finds here. An approach for permission to the landowner is rarely refused, especially when coupled with an offer to clear out the spring and the drainage channel.

Equipment

It will be necessary to have the following equipment: a pair of waders, a rake, a floating sieve, a scoop attached to a long pole, and a detector with a well waterproofed search head. Mark out, as far as possible, a search area. Conduct the search

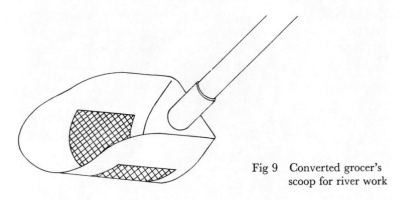

Fig 9   Converted grocer's
scoop for river work

in rows equal to the length of a comfortable sweep across the
marked-out area. When a find is made, extract it with the aid
of a scoop. Try adapting a grocer's-type scoop from which a
three-inch square is cut in the base and replaced with quarter-
inch wire or plastic mesh (Fig 9). The mesh allows the water
to pass through and the solids are retained for examination.
This is best accomplished by tipping the solids into a floating
sieve anchored to a heavy weight by a nylon cord. Never put
too much material into the sieve—about a quarter full should
be the maximum. A floating sieve can easily be made by tying
a quarter-inch mesh garden sieve or a polythene kitchen bowl
with sieve bottom to the inside of a car-tyre inner tube with
non-rotting nylon string (see illustration). The contents of the
sieve can be gently dunked and shaken until the particles of
mud or sand are washed away. Examine the contents very
carefully indeed; work slowly and painstakingly. Gold, brass
and copper will be the easier to recognise as they will retain
something of their original colour. Silver of any age, however,
will almost certainly appear to be black and if the mud is also
black you will have great difficulty in distinguishing the find.

The design of your detector will dictate the depth of water in
which you can operate. Whatever happens do take great care,
in moments of concentration, not to immerse the control box.
It is possible to dispense with the floating sieve if you can
fabricate the scoop described above. Whether you go to all this

A home-made floating sieve

trouble is a matter of personal choice; many of the best finds have been made in shallow water and in ponds or lakes where leisure activities have taken place.

Canals

Some canals such as the Fosse Dyke were constructed during the first century AD and formed part of a waterway system connecting places as far apart as York and Cambridge. Short sections have been built over the centuries to link navigable rivers, but it was the Industrial Revolution that gave tremendous impetus to the growth of waterborne transport and played a significant part in our commercial growth until the railways forced the canals into decline. The navvies—an abbreviation of navigators—were the hard, itinerant construction workers who built the canals. A study of the dates when various sections of canal were opened—it is all well documented —can lead you to find sites of navvies' camps and where they had their own entertainments such as prize fighting, cock fighting, etc. Now, of course, improved road systems take trade from the railways, but leisure demands have made a strong case for the restoration of the canals. Enthusiasts have banded together and by sheer hard work—often fighting bureaucracy—have managed to get considerable stretches reopened and working again. This has meant much dredging

A charming scene on a canal towpath; a likely site for interesting finds (*Mansell Collection*)

and rebuilding of locks and pounds. The work continues by these groups of dedicated people wielding pick and shovel weekend after weekend. Such groups can give information on the past history of their project, and parish records, canal museums and old maps will provide much more. Many of the old public houses which line the canal banks are steeped in the old traditions. Try to form a liaison with a canal restoration group and come to some arrangement regarding finds. They are voluntary workers and need funds for their work so you might be useful to each other, for there are many items of value and interest that could be found when one thinks of the age of these man-made waterways and the commerce they have carried over the years. Towpaths are also worth searching.

Lochs and Lakes

Before passing on to the sea and the coast, it is also worth sparing a thought to the Scottish lochs. Scotland is rich in awe-inspiring scenery and can offer considerable interest to the treasure hunter. Again historical research is vital if success is to follow. The metal detector is not seen so often in this part of Britain and you would normally expect to have to work harder to achieve results. Many finds have been made, however, and at one time the river and stream gravels were the richest source of gold in Britain. In the eighteen hundreds a gold nugget weighing one and a half ounces was found in the Kildonan Burn in Sutherland. You never know your luck— but you will need a special permit for gold prospecting. Medieval coins and pieces of armour are more likely to be the order of the day, however. Many were the battles fought in this part of the world and many too were the escapes and pursuits across the lochs. If you are likely to be spending some time in a particular area, find out all you can about it and, if it looks promising, get the necessary permission to use your detector. The margins of lakes and reservoirs are possibilities also.

Beaches

If you were to ask yourself, your family or any of your acquaintances where they are most likely to have lost some item of cash or jewellery, the chances are that they would say 'On a beach'. Cash, of course, is particularly vulnerable. The beach is one of the few places where people disrobe publicly, albeit under the cover of a towel or in a cramped tent. Having, with considerable difficulty and in the confines of respectability, managed to effect a change into bathing gear, clothes are then rolled up or wrapped in a towel until the reverse procedure is laboriously undertaken. Few people take the precaution of tying up their valuables in a knotted handkerchief. Small wonder then that so much falls into the sand, quickly to get covered up and to disappear.

Even if you do not undress the chances are that you will soon be reclining on the sand or shingle or in a deckchair in a fairly horizontal position. Either way there is a very good chance of your hard-earned cash finding its way out of your pockets. Suitably rested perhaps, a quick game of rounders or cricket will shake out some more cash. Dry sand is almost like liquid

Teignmouth, Devon, in 1907 (*Radio Times Hulton Picture Library*)

in behaviour; items will very quickly get swallowed, particularly if presenting an edge to the sand. A few movements around it and it is buried and the chances of finding it become more remote as the search progresses.

The development of the railway in early Victorian times was instrumental in the growth of the holiday-by-the-sea habit. It continued to grow as standards of living rose with improved wages and holidays. New towns grew up by the seaside and the grand-hotel type of establishment was built for the rich. Lost wealth has been accumulating on the beaches ever since. One does not need much imagination to appreciate how much must be lying there.

Enormous numbers of vessels have been wrecked round our coasts, particularly round the south-west peninsula in the past two thousand years or so. Whilst these will have been well picked over by locals—in some cases, 'wreckers' deliberately lured ships onto rocks—small items may have escaped their clutches and became lodged in crevices in the rocks, or be revealed by the effect of tides, erosion and landslips. When researching wrecks, valuable information can be gleaned from seafaring literature of the period such as the *Nautical Magazine*, trade literature, Lloyds insurance records and the comprehensive Admiralty Index Digest which is kept at the Public Records Office. Piers, breakwaters and groynes act as traps for smaller items carried along by the tides in just the same way that we get our hotspots in the river. Where do we start looking? Being totally surrounded by coastline the scope and choice is limitless. But first, some useful points.

The ideal time to go beachcombing is not on a bright, calm sunny day, but when gales are forecast. The rough weather and high winds will cause the whipped-up seas to move and displace the surface sand and shingle and reveal the hard-packed silt where finds may well lie. The best seasons to go beachcombing are the autumn and winter, October and November often being particularly favourable. The holiday season will be finished and the visitors will have departed;

An autumn search of a beach hut area after the holidaymakers have left

the weather too starts to deteriorate but is still reasonably comfortable as long as one wraps up well. Do study tides—not only the times of high and low water but very particularly their local characteristics. Ask local fishermen about the currents; the price of a pint may prove a very good investment, particularly if it saves your life! Where the foreshore or beach is flat and the tide seems to recede for miles, it gives a false sense of security on the assumption that it must take hours to come in. Nothing is farther from the truth. It can approach very rapidly indeed and the unwary can be cut off before they can appreciate what is happening, particularly if they are engrossed in a search. Watch out for quicksands which can be perilous and lethal. They cannot always be marked because they just come and go, so proceed cautiously and try to get local advice.

Eroded beaches indicate strong tides and currents and provide a good site on which to search. What the treasure hunter will need to know is where the currents are strongest and weakest. The weak areas will be the most likely resting place for finds. Some beaches are subject to fast moving riptides which are caused by the offshore configuration of the seabed and create considerable movement and turnover of sand and shingle. These areas too offer good prospects. There is, of course, absolutely no point in planning a search of the low water mark area if the tide is about to change. Study the tide-tables and then follow the tide out so that your search can be carried out at slack water—but keep an eye on it!

Before moving back up the beach to the trippers' paradise, what are the prospects towards low water mark? Well, quite intriguing in fact. For example, around the shores of the Bay of Tay, Dundee, many gold coins have been found from the treasure fleet which foundered there and sank during a storm in 1651. Only a few years ago, a gold bar was picked up on the beach at Bognor in Sussex; the British Museum assayed it and found that it did, in fact, contain platinum and was probably of South American origin. This was thought to indicate that it could have come from an uncharted Spanish wreck or treasure ship somewhere offshore. Another wreck, that of the *Hindostan* which sank in 1803 off Margate, is thought to be the source of the many old coins found here; seventeenth-century coins indicate yet another, but unknown, wreck in the vicinity. A find on Hayling Island some few years ago was a brass box dug up from the mud which was found to contain seventy-seven sixteenth-century coins. Odd single cannons too have been found hereabouts which would presuppose old wrecks.

The top of Beachy Head is well known for the valuable finds of Roman coins and hoards; therefore it is reasonable to suppose that a thorough search of the whole beach area below should yield results. Selsey, a good example of an eroded fore-shore, offers interesting prospects also. During a period of natural silt clearance, the foundations of an old building were discovered there recently. Searching the most exposed areas at low tide should bring results as a fair proportion of former land is now lost to the sea and currents have deposited coins on the beach. Conversely, of course, a great deal of treasure must lie under thousands of tons of silt which has caused towns such as Sandwich and old fortresses such as nearby Richborough, once at the sea's edge, now to be found some distance inland. The River Wantsum which was nearly two miles wide at its mouth hundreds of years ago and made Thanet into an island is, nowadays, not much more than a ditch running from the Stour to the sea.

Whilst the temptation may be to search around the high water mark where the public congregate, finds of greater historical value are likely to be made below this line. Wrap up well, use all the usual search techniques, protect your detector from salt and do keep a weather eye open for that advancing tide. Your chances of stopping it are no better than King Canute's.

Moving now up the beach, a rather different set of values emerge. Here, the modern beachcomber with his metal detector can, and in many cases actually does, earn a living through recovery of money, jewellery and other personal valuables such as watches and lighters. But spare a thought for the longshoremen and beachcombers who have traditionally supplemented their incomes or even grubbed a living from the pickings on the seashore. The metal detector represents a threat to them. Don't crowd them.

A family outing: beachcombing on a shingle beach

As we saw earlier, a very considerable number of losses takes place through changing of clothes, lounging and sporting activities. In addition there are all the commercial functions such as deck-chair hire, donkey rides, ice cream and shellfish stalls, etc. If, during the season, the positions of these operations are noted, a careful search of the site when the season ends will often produce a bonanza.

Generally, beach activities have not changed much since Victorian times. It is possible to find a fair proportion of Victorian coinage and jewellery among recoveries. Search around beach huts; finds may be modern but the huts are, in all probability, in the same position as in Victorian times. Study old postcards for clues. Punch and Judy shows, particularly between the wars, were a source of wonder and delight to children who, sitting on the sands watching, might lose their pocket money. The showman too would undoubtedly drop the odd coin or two.

Swimming can part bathers from their valuables; let's face it, the sea is rarely really warm in Britain and rings can slip from fingers contracted by the cold. Catches and safety chains can be weakened by the power of the waves.

One of the biggest bugbears of beachcombing has been the large amount of silver paper around, the drink can and, in particular, its pull tab. Depending on the type of detector, these have been a considerable source of lost time and frustration; fortunately the latest type of discriminator detectors are doing much to eliminate this problem.

Sid Clayton, Chairman of the National Association of Metal Detector Clubs, has been a serious and successful beachcomber for over twenty-seven years. At every available opportunity he observes the habits of the sea, studying the movement of the sand in relation to the forces of wind and water. He recalls one particular day when the wind rose to Gale Force 10, and his amazement when he actually saw coins dancing in the wash as the waves pounded against a sea wall. It was a particularly

Fig 10   Effect of wind and tide on distribution of coins in sea

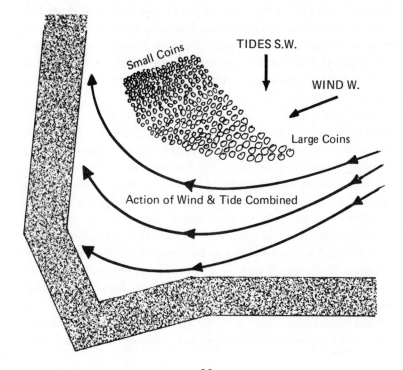

high spring tide with the wind blowing almost directly behind it, propelling the waves a considerable distance beyond the normal high water line. Sid waited with detector at the ready until the wind and tide had dropped and, within two hours, he discovered 528 coins.

The distribution of the coins is of special significance as it demonstrates the action of the waves and currents in carrying objects according to their weight and size—a light object will obviously be carried further than a heavy one (Fig 10).

The study of a section of sandy beach will reveal varying layers or strata. Bear in mind that the action of the waves, particularly in bad weather, and the effect of wind cause constant movement of the surface sand or shingle. Under the top layers of loose sand is hardpacked sand. Over long periods, lost articles come to rest eventually on this hard layer through the movement of the softer sand above it. Recent losses therefore will tend to lie not too far below the surface and then, if not recovered, will gradually sink down. Thus the deeper you dig, the older will be the finds. The best thing is to use a good spade or shovel and a garden sieve although, if the sand is fine, a wire chip frying basket is useful. Apart from ability to discriminate, your detector should have good deep penetration characteristics. It is easy to mark out a search area in the sand unless there is a wind blowing, in which case pegs and string become necessary. Work slowly and carefully and dig fairly deeply. Remember to fill in the holes again; it may be just a beach where it is customary to build sand castles, but leaving deep holes all over the place is not only unsightly but it can be dangerous and it gets us a bad name.

Elizabeth Green is proprietor of a treasure hunting centre in Cardiff. She finds she can go to the same place time and time again with repeated success, and stresses the need to observe and understand the character of a beach and its changing pattern of tides and currents. On one particular beach she found 'shelves' of coins in a spot where steps had led down to the sand from seaside stalls. The action of the waves had piled sand over the steps and buried coins with it; in the space of forty-five minutes nearly 2500 coins were located by four detectors. More coins keep turning up when she returns there.

During the summer season, paying a visit to the beach after the dinner gongs have all been sounded in the guest houses or during rain can be very fruitful as losses will not have had a chance to get buried deeply. These are what might be called short-term or get-rich-quick angles; the long-term aspect requires deeper study. As we have seen, nothing has greater influence on the success of beachcombing than a spell of rough weather. The natural elements will then do a great deal of the hard work for you, exposing patches of beach and hard pack that might ordinarily mean hours of digging. You should be on the spot as soon as you possibly can after a storm. Crashing waves may well have deposited objects higher up the beach than normal and these high tide lines can be worth exploring. Should you discover coins of a period which ordinarily you would not expect to find in a particular search area, it is worth digging and exploring thoroughly since these would hardly likely to have been lost by current holidaymakers. Another useful tip is that an offshore wind, that is one blowing away from the beach, is more favourable than an onshore breeze which tends to cover items up. A wind too which blows in the opposite direction to that which normally prevails has much the same effect. It is, of course, doubtful that you will often find perfect copybook conditions but, the more you study and appreciate the effects of weather, the greater the chances of your success on the beach.

Just one last word on beaches. During recent movements of large quantities of shingle at Dungeness a frightening number of unexploded mortars and similarly lethal objects have turned up. This is a possibility anywhere along our coasts where war-time defences existed or where army exercises have taken place since. Keep an eye open for any object which looks suspicious and report it at once to the police. Do not touch or interfere with it.

91

6 Hoard Prospecting

A hoard is described as 'an accumulation stored away for safe guarding or future use'; to hoard is 'to gather and store away, or hide for future use'. The last few words are important because, as far as the treasure hunter is concerned, they form the basis of a coroner's reasoning in declaring such finds to be treasure trove (see Chapter 10). In other words, the person who concealed the hoard fully intended to return and recover it. What unfortunate circumstances intervened to prevent recovery can only be a matter for conjecture except where known or reported information exists. Often bound up in history, legends handed down over generations or contained in writings, it is the tracing of this sketchy information that forms the basis of hoard hunting. Many hoards have been stumbled on quite accidentally in the course of ploughing, plain coin hunting or whilst looking for something entirely different; this is pure unadulterated luck. What we are concerning ourselves with in this chapter is how to go about searching based on evidence of some kind, preparing the ground by sound detective work and research and then following it through to what we hope will be a successful conclusion.

It may be supposed that most hoards will be old, going back before the establishment of banks in the late seventeen hundreds and early eighteen hundreds. However banks were not really trusted in the earlier days and some people preferred to hide their wealth; it is a fairly common instinct to hoard. The proceeds of burglaries or perhaps even 'hot money' being concealed from the eyes of the Inland Revenue are hidden away; highwaymen often had to conceal their haul quickly in case they were caught red-handed with the damning evidence of their calling. Even so, and making due allowance for the multiplicity of reasons for concealment in more recent periods, hoarding was much more pressing in medieval times and further back still in the Anglo-Saxon and Roman periods.

It is difficult to realise how insecure our forebears were in the Middle Ages. Because of widespread banking facilities and the use of credit cards, cheque books and bank guarantee cards, we do not now have to carry the bulk of our wealth with us when we travel as they did. We even have travellers' cheques and that wonderful standby, in some cases, credit-worthiness. None of these things existed for our ancestors who had to devise what means they could to secure their wealth from the unwelcome attentions of everyone from the invading Roman legions to the highwayman and footpads of the eighteenth and nineteenth centuries. How carefully hoards were hidden depended much on the circumstances; there were those who, having time to consider and ponder the problem, would be able to make concealment very thorough. On the other hand, one can well imagine the panic surrounding the unexpected arrival of Viking plunderers, or that of an un-fortunate Royalist about to be seized by Cromwell's troops. Indeed, there are many stories of hoards buried by Royalists who, as they gradually lost their cause, concealed their wealth so that the Roundheads would not lay hands on it.

The famous diarist Samuel Pepys, Secretary to the Admiralty in the reign of King Charles II, recounted how he tried to move some of his wealth out of London in 1667. The Dutch, as was their unfortunate habit at the time, had sailed up the Thames and burned some of our ships, causing an invasion scare. Pepys sent about £3100 in gold by coach to a place near Huntingdon in the charge of his wife and father. He wrote, 'Pray God give them good passage and good care to hide it . . .' his heart 'being full of fear'. He then sent a Mr Gibson after his wife with yet another thousand pieces. Gibson returned next day unexpectedly bearing ill tidings and the diarist continues, 'He had one of his bags broke, through his breeches, and some pieces dropped out, not many he thinks but . . .'. He seems to have found most of these and Samuel Pepys was happy that nothing worse had happened. Then, waiting till things had died down, he went some four months later to recover his gold where it had been buried in a garden at Buckden where his father lived. Firstly he, his father and his wife had to wait until some visitors had gone and then they set forth 'with a dark lantern, it now being night . . . and there went about my great work to dig up my gold'. As he puts it 'I began heartily to sweat and be angry' since apparently they could not at first remember where it was buried and he worried in case someone had found it. However, at last they located it by 'poking with a spit'. This was not to be the end of the story, for it was then found that the bags had rotted and as he lifted his precious gold pieces the bags broke and deposited the coins all around in the earth and grass. This did not improve his humour and being unsure how much gold there should be it 'made me mad'! The statements of cash deposited also rotted, it seems. Eventually the trio gathered together all they could find. They then had some supper and afterwards set about clearing up. To Pepys' relief he estimated that he had only lost some 'twenty or thirty gold pieces altogether', some of which might be attributed to the hapless Mr Gibson's misadventure. This quite true story contains so many little human traits. It also typifies the very kind of incident which leads to hoards being buried and lost—the difference in this case, of course, being that the owner managed to recover most of it. What happened to those missing coins though? They might still be there.

A very great deal has been written about where hoards have been found in the past and these make fascinating reading and form a positive encouragement to treasure and hoard hunters. These books are available to the reader and it is not proposed to list these sites here for, apart from drawing attention to a particular area as being possibly lucrative, such reported

King Henry VIII's Charter for Walton Fair; careful research into old documents and maps reveals potential sites for interesting finds hoards have already been discovered. We are much more concerned with finding others. Indeed, a list of areas worth searching might appear to be an enlarged edition of one of the motoring gazetteers. Any town, city or area of the British Isles, whether it be woodland, scrubland or whatever, could be a good prospect. It is the technique of research, the patience and remorseless attention to detail, in much the same way that the successful detective puts a crime puzzle together, that eventually bears fruit. It could take years depending on the follow-up research involved as some legends go back for centuries.

Lord Bolton's estate, old Basing House near Basingstoke in Hampshire, is very much fancied as a hiding place for a hoard or hoards worth millions of pounds. Unfortunately for the treasure hunter, however, as the area is scheduled as an ancient monument and therefore protected, it is not possible to go prospecting unless supervised. The story goes that the fifth Marquis of Winchester finally succumbed to the Roundheads in 1645 after a siege lasting three years. The Roundheads carried off loot reputedly worth nearly a quarter of a million pounds. It was strongly rumoured that the Marquis had taken steps to conceal the bulk of his treasure and that he had spread it around the area. Some credence is given to this theory by the discovery of a fortune in treasure, thought to belong to the nobleman, when the Basingstoke Canal was being excavated. More treasure is thought to be concealed under the old ruined chapel on the estate. Berkshire, being a Royalist stronghold during the Civil War, is thought to contain a large number of hoards and hidden fortunes, particularly in the Thames Valley. At Caversham Heights there is the famous St Anne's Well where it is reputed that Cavaliers concealed their wealth.

There is some fact to support the story of King John losing his baggage in the Wash in 1216, although controversy has always surrounded it. As was the royal custom of those days, King John was on a fund-raising tour of East Anglia. It appears that he had done very well from the wealthy noblemen and abbeys and was carrying a considerable fortune when he decided to stop at Kings Lynn overnight whilst en route for Lincoln. The next day disaster overtook him and his baggage train. To save a long journey inland a short cut was taken across the low lying marshland called the Cross Keys Wash. This was wide and usually quite safe and a known ford. Progress was, however, slow and the train was overtaken by an unusually high tide which drowned most of the animals and men. King John's immense treasure was lost too in an area, so legend has it, about three miles north-east of St Mary's Church, Sutton. What one might term an 'accidental' hoard but there are some authorities who do not accept the treasure story at all, maintaining instead that the tale was a political expedient.

There are literally hundreds of stories told covering every county and period concerning hoards and buried treasure. Many, however, may never have reached official ears. Equally there is a little doubt that there is a hoard in, or near to, your own area. It may not be necessary to go too far afield; many of the hoards found have been discovered within a few miles of the finder's home. Some have even been made in chimneys and under floorboards. Builders frequently discover 'nest eggs', particularly when carrying out alterations to medieval properties. Workmen carrying out some plumbing repairs in York some few years ago found an old bronze pot blocking a drain. It contained a large number of coins of the Edward I period. Many old buildings are listed and protected nowadays, and are not often demolished unless hopelessly beyond restoration. If, however, you should see or hear of such a demolition taking place it would be well worth trying to obtain permission from the contractors to carry out a search before things go too far. Avoid any subsequent disputes concerning ownership of finds by having a written agreement set out first.

Attics are always worth a search—look for a money box nailed to a joist or to rafters. Examine floorboards for signs of irregular boards. When the detector is passed over a floor there is usually a regular pattern caused by nails in the joists

Searching the ruins of a
derelict house

or beams; anything showing up which breaks the pattern
should be investigated. Pass the detector over brick walls and
chimney breasts. In the likely event of not having an old plan
from which to work, look for indications of bricking up,
changes in wall thickness or any clue which might reveal an
attempt to make alterations. It is not unknown for concealed
rooms and priest's holes to be discovered. The old style of
timber box construction used in Tudor times allowed a lot of
latitude for concealment as there were often no brick walls
as we know them today. Cellars also often prove fruitful.

Moving outside, outhouses and old stabling should be carefully searched, floors, walls and around roof joists in particular.
It was often thought safer to conceal a treasure hoard by
burying it in the garden or grounds. There it would not be
threatened by fire and the chances of discovery would be
reduced. An area which consistently throws up single coins of
about the same period should always be given close attention—
they could be part of a hoard.

Never neglect an opportunity to study title maps and old town maps or plans and then to compare them with more modern ones. Libraries, town halls or city archives are the places to visit, or you could go to the Public Records Office. It is quite incredible on occasions how far back records go and what amazing detail they contain. By making an exhaustive study of your chosen locality it should be possible to build up a picture of history and tradition extending back over many years. This information together with local legend and gossip will form a basis on which to work. Some local newspapers go back as much as two centuries. From time to time they publish extracts from much earlier editions, so there is a mine of information just waiting to be consulted. The custodians are usually very proud of it and more than pleased to give help and advice.

Eventually you will need the co-operation of people when you seek permission to search. You must be prepared to come up against a stonewall and point-blank refusal. However, if you explain your painstaking research and can arouse sufficient interest in the owner, he or she may become as enthusiastic as you are, particularly if you have managed to produce tangible evidence that there is a very strong possibility of Lord Some-body-or-Other's long-lost millions being around and that they will receive a fifty per cent share if it is found. Some are natural diplomats and some are not, of course, but most people are quite reasonable and helpful if approached in the right spirit.

We have looked at possible reasons for the existence of hoards, where they might be found in buildings and how we might start to research using all the local knowledge and information we can muster. But as we saw in Chapter 1, many hoards have been unearthed in open country and farmland. Most of these finds have been stumbled on by accident as will always prove to be the case. To find a concealed hoard out in the country, unless supported by exacting research, offers very long odds indeed. Just chasing a hunch will rarely offer much in the way of reward when one considers the astronomical odds. Talking to farmers and their workers, villagers or inn-keepers may give a useful clue. On hearing for example that 'old Harry turned up a few pieces of pottery the other day when he was ploughing up there in Five Acres', a follow-up would be well advised; hoards were often contained with pots or cauldrons. Be careful you have not stumbled on an arch-aeological site however. It is always possible to check this with the local archaeological society—the librarian or museum curator will put you in touch. You can then compare notes on the position of the site as shown on the Ordnance Survey map. This is always advisable, particularly if a small find of medieval or Roman coins or artefacts might indicate, through close dating, the existence of such a site. Otherwise, and subject to the usual agreement being made with the farmer, you can continue to search further. Remember that the coins may have got scattered so widen your search area.

One of the most exciting hoard finds was made using a BFO-type detector which only cost £25. Mrs Dorothy Harrison and her son-in-law, Mr Arthur Greensmith, recovered nearly three thousand valuable Roman silver and bronze coins worth something approaching £30,000 from farmland near Lincoln in 1976. Lincoln—known by the Romans as Lindun—was an important centre of their influence. Mrs Harrison and Mr Greensmith were approached by a farmer who told them that he had found evidence of Roman pottery in a field next to a main track; as long as they did not damage crops, he would be pleased for them to carry out a search of the area. This they did in a systematic manner for several evenings and also at weekends under the farmer's direction. To start with there were few finds of significance but the signs were encouraging. A further week passed; then, with that inexplicable feeling of being lucky, Arthur jokingly said to his father-in-law 'We'll bring you home the pot tonight!' They set off and a couple of hours later they were filling bag after bag with coins from a broken Roman pot, the neck of which had doubtless been damaged during ploughing. Some of the coins had spilled out

A selection of well preserved coins from the hoard found by Dorothy Harrison and her son-in-law Arthur Greensmith

and had been scattered. The detector easily picked up these coins which were near to the surface, but then Mrs Harrison decided to recheck the hole where she located the main pot about one foot down. Enlisting the help of the family with trowels, the complete hoard was recovered before darkness and the rest of the evening was spent counting up their good fortune. The hoard was reported to the police next day who made arrangements for the coins to be identified by the British Museum and for the coroner's office to hold an inquest. The following evening the families returned to the site to completely restore it and carefully replant any disturbed seedlings, thus honouring their promise to the farmer and the treasure hunter's code of practice.

The Lincoln city coroner declared the hoard to be treasure trove and ruled that the British Museum should take charge of the coins until they decided if they should purchase the coins from the finders. The British Museum discovered that the majority of the coins, known as 'folles', were minted in the reign of Constantine the Great, dating from AD309 to AD317. The inquest also dealt with yet another find which Mrs Harrison and Mr Greensmith made later. This was eight coins of the earlier period AD77 to AD270. In this case the coins were in all probability lost and were not, therefore, treasure trove and in consequence belonged to the finders.

Many of our farmhouses and farm buildings are quite old. Because of their remoteness they were frequently chosen as hiding places and bolt holes for people fleeing from persecution. During the period of the Civil War the farmers and yeomen were often sympathetic to the Royalist cause and gave shelter and protection to their followers. They may well have concealed small hoards, with or without their host's knowledge. Here again, if permission can be obtained, is a good opportunity to unearth something of value which the owner perhaps had not the remotest idea could have existed in the house in which he had spent his boyhood and life.

Hoard hunting is not like coin hunting round fairgrounds or on the sandy shore of the seaside holiday resort. You can spend months, even years, on research and whilst this will bring its own rewards in terms of interest, it can all come to naught, but the experience gained is usually more than beneficial and will throw up many useful by-products. Perhaps it is not wise to so totally dedicate yourself to one such project that it becomes an obsession to the exclusion of all else. You become stale and sometimes frustrated and tend to neglect all the other forms of treasure hunting that give the enthusiast so much pleasure. Let the project remain an on-going thing and gradually add to the material being built up. It is the surest way of picking up the trail that may even lead to King John's treasure but, be warned, highly motivated people have been searching for it for a long time now—without much luck!

7 Archaeological Co-operation and Record Keeping

In 1976 a one-day conference was held in Bournemouth when archaeologists put their point of view to metal detector users. There was justifiable criticism and valid comment such as that in some cases ancient monuments were being violated, archaeological damage done, landowners' permission not being sought and that many discoveries were going unrecorded. In other words, all those very points which have been laboured throughout these pages. The conference helped to clear the air and engender a new spirit of co-operation. In March 1977 a joint exercise was carried out and the following press release was issued by Dorset County Council:

ARCHAEOLOGISTS AND TREASURE HUNTERS WORK TOGETHER

The general horror felt by archaeologists towards metal-detector users is now well known. In very many cases this is justified since scheduled ancient monuments are violated, archaeological damage is done, landowners' permissions are not sought and many discoveries go unrecorded.

In Dorset efforts are being made to stop the indiscriminate and irresponsible use of detectors. Last year a one-day conference was held in Bournemouth when local archaeologists explained to detector-users why they were so concerned.

Since then discussions have continued between arch-

aeologists and the Bournemouth and District Treasure
Hunting Club. The Club's code of conduct requires that
landowners' permission is sought; archaeological sites and
ancient monuments are not interfered with; archaeologists
are informed of any site to be worked; all items of historical
value are plotted and that museums are informed of items
found. The Club works only on ploughed land.

A newly discovered site under arable land in Purbeck has
given the Club and local archaeologists the opportunity to
carry out a joint exercise in field-work suggested at the

Philip Connolly and members of the Bournemouth and District Treasure
Hunting Club—the Club which has done so much to establish a
co-operative working relationship with local archaeologists

Bournemouth meeting. On Sunday 13 March Dorset County Council's Archaeological Officer, Laurence Keen, organised the day to consist of the systematic collection of all surface finds by walking the field, followed by the use of detectors to compare both results.

During the field walking by the sixteen Club members substantial quantities of pottery, as well as a few Roman coins and a brooch, were collected. Later the Club, using detectors, found a lot more coins and another brooch. The positions of all the coins and brooches were plotted. It was significant that modern coins were often deeper than the Roman ones, in no case more than 4 inches.

During discussion it was agreed by all who had taken part that the collection of all surface finds was necessary to interpret the site and the plotting of pottery and metal objects was necessary to see if there was any concentration of items. For the archaeologist it was significant that the coins found by the detectors reinforced the date suggested by the coins found on the surface, and that it could be shown that no archaeological damage had been done.

The Bournemouth and District Treasure Hunting Club is, no doubt, much more enlightened about archaeological matters than most individuals and other clubs and the suggestion that a national association of clubs is formed will probably be welcomed by archaeologists if a code of conduct like the Bournemouth Club's is to be followed.

Concentrating on the plotting of finds and recording of information from ploughed sites which are not recorded in the archaeological record, together with a responsible attitude to archaeology, will add considerably to the body of archaeological information. But the organisation of this sort of activity implies that clubs alone can cope with it and the Bournemouth Club is hoping that individuals will consider joining a local club.

The Bournemouth Club's concern for the protection of known and scheduled sites is now well demonstrated by its surveillance of Maiden Castle and Badbury Rings, from where lone-wolf detector-users have been turned off. This recent experiment in Dorset shows that archaeologists and metal detector-users can meet on common ground.

In all, it turned out to be a very worthwhile project and offers many useful examples of the way in which treasure hunting should be approached—with responsibility, planning, plotting and recording, and with co-operation which surely, at the end of the day, must be to the common good. There is room for both interests.

The metal detector user's point of view was expressed by another club member in *Coin Monthly* in January 1977:

As in every hobby there is someone to upset the applicant, with numismatists it is the people who buy and sell coins with their own 'grading system', and with metal detector users it is the lone rangers who have bought their machines with one purpose, to make money at any cost to archaeological sites and the rest of the countryside.

I would like to point out that we, as an organised club of long standing, have never been to an archaeological site except for a couple of occasions when requested to do so by archaeologists themselves. On both occasions we were of great use, and it is a pity that this fraternisation does not occur more often.

We have made public our finds at functions supporting church fund raising and have given lectures to numismatic associations and evening institutes.

If there has got to be legislation against metal detector users, let some way be found of legislating against the 'cowboys' and not against the organised clubs whose rules forbid the detecting of sites without the landowner's permission.

H. A. Nicholson, Antiquity Research Association
Cottingham, Humberside

This does not suggest that responsible treasure hunters should not continue to work alone and, of course, a large number do and will continue to do so. It does not mean either that every little find has to be reported. What is being referred to is the need to co-operate closely over the question of indiscriminate and irresponsible use of detectors on sites of archaeological significance. One difficulty is that archaeological sites as such are not all clearly marked or defined. Play safe—it is only necessary to ask the local society whose secretary's address can always be obtained from the museum, town hall or parish offices. This may sound a bit of a bind but remember that if we are to be allowed to have a reasonably free rein in the future, it is a small price to pay now. A word too to museum authorities. Treat treasure hunters fairly. Some have felt bitter because, having taken their finds to their local museum, they have in extreme cases never heard of them again or, in others, received recompense which is ridiculously low.

The views of the Department of the Environment were expressed in a letter from Mr R. L. Long, Head of News, Information Directorate, which appeared in the *Cambridge Evening News* in autumn 1976:

> The use of metal detectors to search for buried coins and other 'treasure' causes great anxiety to archaeologists generally as they foresee the devastation of many archaeological sites. But it is not the use of the detectors themselves which is harmful but the disturbance of the ground surface.
>
> An archaeologist investigates a site scientifically, layer by layer, recording objects found in each layer and attempting to establish a chronology for each feature. Once the layers of a site have been disturbed by an inexperienced digger, even slightly, the important evidence they could have revealed may be lost forever.
>
> There are, of course, many places where the use of detectors and any subsequent digging would do little harm— on beaches or the foreshores of tidal waters, for example. It

is not illegal to dig on land other than sites sceduled as ancient monuments, subject to the consent of the owner. The most important archaeological sites are, of course, scheduled under Section 12 of the Ancient Monuments Consolidation and Amendment Act 1913.

The practicality of banning or controlling the use of metal detectors has been considered more than once, but there are legitimate uses for these devices and the effective enforcement of control measures would be almost impossible. An attempt to impose restrictions might in fact lead to concealment of finds rather than prevent the use of detectors.

Even if the use of metal detectors were to be controlled there is the difficult question of who should be licensed to have detectors. Nobody is agreed on who is a professional archaeologist and who is an amateur treasure hunter. The extremes can be differentiated but there is a grey area in the middle.

The Department of the Environment does not favour the banning or controlling of metal detectors by legislation but believes that the most useful action lies rather in other directions. The first is in continuing to educate the public to appreciate the damage which treasure hunting can do. The second is enlisting the interest and goodwill of landowners and, where appropriate, in assisting them, by agreement, in keeping trespassers away from valuable sites. A particularly useful contribution in both respects can be made by archaeologists acting through their local societies and other organisations.

A fine example of archaeologist/detector-user co-operation comes from Norfolk, where the Caister by-pass was to pass within a few hundred yards of a partly excavated Roman town —an area of great archaeological importance. A detector agent and a journalist, members of the Norfolk Archaeological Rescue Group (NARG) recruited volunteers to search the route and had a crash course in recording techniques from local archaeologists. Aerial photographs showed crop marks, the route of a possible road, the harbour development; these were transferred to maps.

A carefully planned programme was thrown into disarray when the date for work to commence on the by-pass was brought forward. Idle talk of forming a society of detector owners was crystallised into action; the Norfolk and Suffolk Metal Detecting Society was established with the five prime stated aims:

1. To encourage the responsible use of metal detectors.
2. To provide a pool of detector information and expertise.
3. To maintain and, if possible, improve the present excellent local relationship between metal detector users and the archaeological staffs of the Norfolk and Suffolk Museums and Archaeological Units.

The site archaeologist supervising Norfolk and Suffolk Metal Detecting Society members at work on the Caister by-pass (*Anderson, Great Yarmouth*)

4. To embody a group of experienced detector users. This can undertake, as a club function, the systematic search of a potentially fruitful area, with accurate plotting of all finds; or be available to archaeologists in the field should they ask for help.

5. To foster in all members a basic knowledge and appreciation of the best archaeological principles and practice.

The Society's membership card carries this signed agreement: 'I agree to abide by the laid-down Code of Conduct for users of metal detectors and act in a manner that will maintain the Society's good name'. The Assistant Keeper of Archaeology at the Castle Museum, Norwich, agreed to be the Society's consultant.

A site archaeologist supervised the Society members' work; he ordered the wearing of fluorescent waistcoats when the potential danger of massive earthmoving machinery and detector users with headphones clamped to their ears became apparent. Varied finds include coins from Roman times to the present day, part of a Bronze Age axe head, trade tokens, Roman and Anglo-Saxon jewellery, some pottery; all have been faithfully recorded and sent to NARG headquarters where the Archaeological Field Unit is housed.

From this important operation, the implications for the future are obvious. Norfolk archaeologists are aware that a high proportion of detector users are responsible people deeply interested in local history, not vandals with the gleam of instant profit in their eyes.

The Committee for Nautical Archaeology is carrying out a wreck survey in order to collect information leading to knowledge of old trade routes, sizes and construction of ships, armaments and contents of cargoes, and ask that relevant information is reported to them. Obviously, this largely applies to divers making finds on the seabed, but the discovery of large numbers of coins or ship's artefacts in an area may suggest the presence of a nearby wreck. Please report significant finds to the Committee for Nautical Archaeology, Institute of

Archaeology, 31–34 Gordon Square, London WC1.

To many of us the idea of keeping records smacks of bureaucracy, but there is a world of difference somehow between having to do it because of official demand, and doing it voluntarily for one's own benefit. Why bother to keep records? The answer is really very simple—to accumulate and store information that will eventually, hopefully, produce statistics which will be useful in the future. This can have a two-fold benefit; firstly to ourselves in providing useful back-up material in planning future search operations, and secondly, in assisting local or even national archaeological interests in building up historical information.

Before dealing with the recording of finds, a few words on identification are necessary. Obviously, correct identification in the first instance is the key and at least some degree of restoration may be necessary before identification can be attempted (see Chapter 8). There are many books, all written by acknowledged experts in their subject, to which you can refer—a selection is listed under Further Reading on p 139. We have an excellent library system—do use it; you will no doubt also start to build up your own library to cover your particular reference needs. If however your find is not easily recognised, seek the help of your local museum; you should do so in any case if you find is suspected to be of significance.

Before we have objects to identify however, we have got to find them and this is where our record keeping starts. Having considered your project and researched it, on arrival at the site you should sketch a reasonably accurate plan of it, taking care to mark in position trees and other natural objects. These will form useful reference points and will be of great assistance if and when you decide to return to the site in the future. Your site should be marked out in workable strips; then as each coin or article is found, it is recorded on the plan, in order to see whether a distinct pattern emerges. You do not have to go into too much detail and you can quite easily evolve your own system of symbols. Categorise by broad dating, say fifty-year periods, and identify on the record by use of key symbols. At the end of the day you should have some sort of picture; this could perhaps reveal a preponderance of Victorian coins, or even Roman. In the case of the latter, this information could be of great interest to the local archaeological society or museum. Having concluded the search, the completed plan should be filed for future reference. It is surprising how a return visit to a site previously searched will produce much more, and comparison of the new plan with the old could prove very interesting. It could throw up faults in search technique for example. Silver, being heavier than copper, usually finds its way down to a deeper level over a period of years; if your plan revealed that you had only succeeded in locating copper coins, then the chances are that your search technique was at fault. You were not properly interpreting those more subtle signals, or perhaps you were going round too quickly. Your record keeping is thus serving another very practical purpose.

From the basic plan outlined, yet more statistics can be built up—it all depends to what degree you like doing this sort

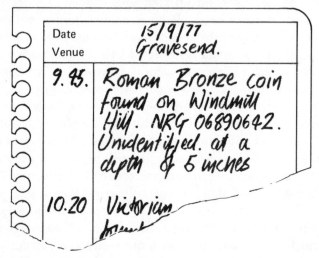

Fig 11　Sample page from a logbook

of exercise. It is possible to produce another type of chart on which the finds are enumerated, categorised and even evaluated. To some treasure hunters it is important for them to know how many coins or objects they unearthed in any particular year, where they found them, and their value, and so to quantify their progress and measure their efficiency.

Many people like to keep a logbook (Fig 11) and from this information to build up a card index system cross-referencing finds under different subjects as well as geographically; any finds made personally, by other club members, and those reported in the press or on radio or television, can be recorded to build up information and suggest future areas of search. Detector response, weather conditions, depth of find, etc, can be recorded, and comparisons of population figures and land use in the area can be noted. By recording finds in a proper systematic way, much useful information can be gathered together which, if interpreted intelligently, can be of considerable use. The next stage is to store and display your finds.

8 Restoring, Cleaning and Displaying Finds

There are several attitudes towards items that have been recovered and it rather depends on what kind of person you are as to what happens to them. Circumstances too will dictate their ultimate destination—whether disclosure is necessary, whether the item is rare and worthy of donation to the local museum, whether the item is sold or retained, after being restored, for one's own collection.

Many treasure hunters are collectors by nature. They get enormous pleasure and interest from their finds, displaying and cataloguing them, recording their history and showing them to friends. Finds should be restored in a proper manner, not just to display them but to protect them too. Some pieces, having been isolated from air for long periods—perhaps centuries—quickly deteriorate if not suitably protected. Conversely of course you might have to do very little, like Mr Hart from North Wales. Searching around an old coaching house he got very positive signals and found an almost brand-new motorcycle which had been stolen only three weeks before and had been buried by the thief. Definitely the sort of find that one should disclose!

Resist the temptation to try to clean a find on site; even rubbing it between your fingers can mark an otherwise perfect specimen. In very simple terms, anything suspected to be rare should not be tampered with; great damage could easily be done by using a wrong cleaning technique and the value of the find be considerably diminished. Take it to the curator of the local museum. One can often see natural atmospheric tainting on very old coins, particularly noticeable on Roman silver-bronze coins which acquire a green discolourisation called patina. This natural coating actually enhances the value of the coin, so you can see the sense of not interfering with rare finds before you know more about them unless, of course, you are an expert yourself. Coins which have become worn or slightly defaced through circulation are found much more often than those in mint or proof condition and their numismatic value is consequently less; in an attempt to restore their lustre, amateur collectors often ruin their pieces by rubbing them up excessively.

The corrosion of a metal object is caused by chemicals which, through contact with the metal, form a new compound. This process can be neutralised by removing this chemical or by the chemical becoming exhausted. For example, coins buried in the ground will continue to corrode until they have neutralised those chemicals around them and with which they are in contact. This aspect of corrosion is important for two main reasons as far as it affects the performance of a detector; as the coin corrodes its metallic content is spread out and thus presents a larger surface area to the detector's search head. The coin is therefore easier to detect at greater depths than a more recently buried coin. The other factor is that, after a time, the older coin will cease to corrode; damage then occurs when the coin comes into contact with oxygen in the air.

In order to assist identification, it is often necessary to remove loose surface dirt and earth. To do this soak the piece in soapy water; do not use a detergent or bleach as anything at all caustic can do untold damage. Then, with an old soft toothbrush, lightly go over the surface with great care. It should then be possible to identify the find. If moderate cleaning only is necessary here are a few techniques for different types of metal.

Gold

There are many varying degrees of purity in gold, which will affect the amount of corrosion. The purer the gold, the slower the deterioration and corrosion and even the most acid of soils will not appreciably harm gold of high quality and purity. Usually all that is needed is a light wash in soapy water with a soft brush and a careful rinse, when it will be restored to all its former glory. A lovely sight!

Silver

Silver is not quite so simple but, unless found in extremes of acid or alkaline conditions, silver items are normally in a fair state of preservation. Corrosion ordinarily takes the form of accretions of silicates or carbonates. Soaking in a 10 per cent solution of ammonia and then lightly brushing with the soft toothbrush will usually have the desired effect after a thorough rinse to avoid tarnishing. To maintain a nice finish, always be careful to avoid cheap abrasive types of polish. An occasional dip in Silverdip and a light rub with cotton wool should be all that is necessary to maintain its appearance.

Copper

Copper, rather like silver, is affected principally by sulphates, carbonates and silicates which again can be removed in a solution of ammonia. An alternative is vinegar or lemon juice (including rind) or oxalic acid. Rinse well and dry carefully.

Brass

Brass items are often found although these are more likely to be trading tokens than coins. Trading tokens, which are popular collector's pieces, were used in the seventeenth and eighteenth centuries by companies and employers in lieu of wages. Brass

116

is easily cleaned with lemon juice or vinegar or a mild brass polish.

Modern Coins

Modern coins feature most prominently in the average treasure hunter's list of finds and will probably be cupro-nickel although some categories of modern coinage, depending on date and consequent level of silver therein, are well worth watching out for. Go through your finds of modern coins carefully therefore before you decide to buy something with them. In any case they will probably want cleaning and the simplest way, as well as being the quickest and most effective, is to soak the coins in a solution of common vinegar and a little salt for ten minutes or so and then agitate them to remove the surface dirt. In the main the coins will only be worth face value and it will not particularly matter if they are scratched or bent as they should still be honoured at the bank. Just use the appropriate solution for cleaning, dry them and that is all there is to it.

Electrolysis

To remove substantial corrosion on finds represents a different problem and requires a much more scientific approach. One of the best methods is the process of electrolysis; most treasure hunting shops sell the necessary apparatus.

Some objects will require substantial restoration where corrosion is advanced. Often the most difficult decision is to know when to stop—one can always remove more material but it is quite impossible to replace it! Great care is therefore a prerequisite and constant supervision should be maintained. Electrolysis may be simply described as the breaking up of a chemical compound by electricity. Particles are removed from the surface of the item being cleaned by passing an electric current between the item being cleaned and another metal object, both immersed in an acid solution; loosened particles

117

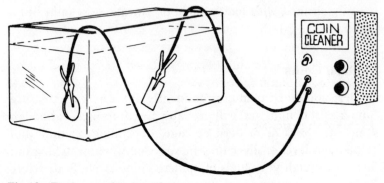

Fig 12 Equipment for electrolysis

transfer themselves to the other piece of metal. The rate of transference is dictated by the strength of the acid solution and of the current being passed. The greater these are, the faster the process.

Equipment with the facility of a variable electrical output gives greater flexibility, particularly in the final stages of cleaning when the process needs to be slowed down. The solution commonly used is one of one teaspoonful of citric acid, half a teaspoonful of salt and one and a half pints of water. Use a glass container of about two pints' capacity unless cleaning a large item; there is a risk of all kinds of electrical troubles if a metal container is used—glass is much safer. A low current of only three to six volts is used. The negative wire is secured to the object being cleaned by means of a crocodile clip, and the positive wire it attached to the other piece of metal to complete the circuit—preferably by a one-inch strip of stainless steel (Fig 12). When the object has been cleaned sufficiently, it should be removed from the solution whilst the current is still flowing. This will ensure that it is actively discharging which prevents tainting from the contaminated solution. Bearing in mind that the current is still on, care must be taken of course to see that the two electrodes do not come into contact with each other or a dead short circuit will occur. Never use the same solution for different metals, and wash all equipment immediately after use. When cleaning silver items by this method, hydrogen sulphide may be produced. Its 'rotten eggs' odour can paralyse the sense of smell and, being a heavy gas, can remain at floor level and be slow to disperse. Adequate ventilation is essential.

Electro-chemical Cleaning

A further method which is just as effective but not so easy to handle or control, is to boil the object in a 15 per cent caustic soda solution, together with sacrificial zinc filings or aluminium foil or pieces. It is a messy and dangerous process and requires considerable care if skin burns are to be avoided. If you are unlucky or careless enough to spill any of the solution on yourself, it should be washed off immediately in water. As with electrolysis, never use the same solution for different metals. Always work next to a sink if you possibly can and wash up the equipment thoroughly as soon as it is finished with. Further corrosion or need for cleaning can be avoided by varnishing or lacquering, but this tends to give an artificial look.

Summary of Do's and Don'ts

1. Never leave any chemicals within the reach of children.
2. Do not use the same solution for different metals.
3. Do not use detergent-type powders, only pure soap.
4. Do not try to clean rare or valuable finds yourself—always seek expert help and advice.
5. Don't be impatient; delay attempts to clean your finds or carry out investigation until you get home.
6. Always wear safety glasses when working with acid solutions and ensure plenty of ventilation to disperse fumes.

Storage and Display

Whilst there is nothing to beat a properly constructed cabinet with drawers for the display of coins, these are expensive and you may have to resort to cheaper ways of exhibiting them. Whatever you do, however, never stack your coins—keep them well ventilated and in as dry a place as possible. While plastic envelopes are useful when showing coins and other small items to friends as they prevent them being marked, condensation can form and cause corrosion. Remove them from the plastic before too long and store them in brown manilla envelopes, or maybe utilise slide boxes. A useful by-product of keeping records of your finds, where and when they were discovered, etc, for research purposes, is to provide interesting data which, if imaginatively mounted, can add to the effectiveness and professionalism of your display. Small showcases can be made of balsa wood lined with foam plastic or felt, or finds could be held in position by pins on polystyrene tiles. A metal detector user can take a justifiable pride in displaying and labelling his finds.

9 Other Avenues of Thought

With the number of detector owners increasing daily, more and more people manage to earn a living from treasure hunting or at least comfortably supplement their income. A successful punter with a winning streak may turn his thoughts to dependence on it for his livelihood, but it is a well recognised fact that there is a considerably larger number of successful bookies than punters. It is much the same if one ever considers making a living from treasure hunting. True professionals and professionalism go together and entails total dedication, having a flair for the job and a no-nonsense approach.

Many treasure hunters will go coin hunting and make enough money to recover the operating costs—batteries, repairs and maintenance—and even to recoup the capital cost of their equipment. Some, as we have seen, really hit the jackpot and make a small fortune, by accident or by sheer hard research work and thorough scanning. Most achieve average success and enough encouragement to carry on; after all, we are not all looking for the same thing in our hobby.

Sometimes a very useful and positive service can emerge that gives benefit all round. Mr and Mrs Paestow have a lapidary supplies business in Broadstairs, a business which originated out of their joint interest in collecting semi-precious and decorative stones. This, another branch of treasure hunting, led them eventually to expanding their interest into the field of metal detectors, becoming agents and stockists. One summer afternoon, an incident occurred which added a very useful side to their business. They were beachcombing locally with a detector when some foreign students became interested in their

Mr Paestow of Broadstairs operating his 'Recovery Service'; note the carefully marked-out search area

activities. After a chat the students went back to their game of football and the Paestows to their searching. In the rough and tumble of the game one of the students suddenly missed his watch. At that moment the new 'Recovery Service' was born—necessity being the mother of invention! The Paestows were asked for their help and, mapping out a search area methodically, the detector did not take too long to locate the missing watch which, due to the disturbance of the soft sand by the football game, was already ten inches down. The student was quite naturally delighted, and, being the sound businessman he is, Mr Paestow immediately saw the potential of offering a service to the large number of visitors who annually flock to the area. The jungle drums and local grapevine spread the word and, before too long, the Paestows were in demand and being called out more often then the nearby Ramsgate life-boat!

The 'Recovery Service' is properly run on a sound business footing with costed scale charges and conditions of acceptance.

An hourly charge is made for example and this has got to be cost-effective and to be sufficient to deter timewasters. However, if an article is worth more than £50, ten per cent of the value is paid if found. Such valuables are usually insured and recovery costs can ordinarily be recovered from the insurers. Whatever the arguments regarding insurance, there are certainly not any arguments from Mr Paestow's clients who are usually delighted to be reunited with their possessions and he gets great pleasure from finding and handing back the lost property and seeing the beaming smiles. A large number of articles have been recovered, mainly wedding rings, bracelets and engagement rings including a diamond ring worth about £500. Keys are frequently lost and cause many worried people to seek help from the service; a large number of keys are always turning up on the beach, most unclaimed. This service helps the public to understand what metal detectors are all about and what they are now capable of; good public relations.

If you own a metal detector, you could find yourself in demand and assisting in some unusual project. The Brenzett Aeronautical Museum was founded in August 1972 with the object of recovering aircraft shot down during the Battle of Britain over the Romney Marshes. Appropriately the Museum is sited where, later in 1944, the area served as an advanced airfield for American Mustangs of the Royal Air Force during the doodle-bug menace. The Museum is staffed by the Amalgamated Ashford and Tenterden Recovery Groups who do not receive any financial reward for their considerable effort to display their finds to the public. Proceeds from admission charges to the Museum are ploughed back into the costs of recovering more material for display and any surplus at the end of the year is divided equally between the RAF Benevolent Fund and Polish Air Force Charities. Altogether a very worthwhile project.

The author was asked by the group to assist in the recovery of a Hurricane that had crashed at Melon Farm in the Marshes. The Lancaster family, who had lived there during those turbulent wartime days, notified the Museum that they had witnessed the crash of a Polish pilot. Only five years of age at the time, Brian Lancaster recalls the pilot, knocking at the farmhouse door, flashing a row of gold-capped teeth in a big smile. The inevitable tea being served, the family then chatted with the pilot until a pickup arrived to take him back to base.

The location and recovery of crashed planes requires immeasurable patience and is often dependent on information gathered from the public, documents or photographs and the like. With the help of a 1948 aerial photograph, the Museum's project leader, John Whinney, was able to narrow the location down to two fields. From such photos, a crash site can often be identified by disturbance in vegetation or soil discolouration.

During the late sixties, the government decided that disclosure of the whereabouts of crashed planes no longer

The author helping in the search for a World War II crashed Hurricane in sticky conditions

The tail wheel with partially inflated tyre and remnants of other tyres from the crashed Hurricane

threatened the nation's security and effectively ownership of the planes passed to the landowners from the Ministry of Defence. The present owner of Melon Farm, Mr Cragg, gave permission for the Recovery Group to carry out a preliminary search of the area and subsequently donated all the finds to the Museum.

The preliminary search party, using metal detectors, located several metal objects which were identified as parts of the fuselage, but failed to actually pinpoint the crash spot. Patience being one of the best weapons in a treasure hunter's armoury, John Whinney returned a month later as the field had by then been ploughed. Several hours of meticulous searching elapsed before he was finally able to establish the wreck's precise location which he then recorded on an Ordnance Survey map. A mechanical digger was hired and the serious business of recovery was begun, each fragment being carefully unearthed and catalogued. All large parts were placed to one side and methodically cleaned whilst another group carried on searching the spoilage in case any small items had been missed. Here a

125

problem revealed shortcomings in the type of detector we were using. The soil around the engine was saturated with engine oil which contained minute metal particles. The metal detectors we were using could not be tuned in these conditions because the metallic content overloaded the electromagnetic search field, simulating severe ground effect. Until the availability of a ground exclusion IB detector, this part of the search had to be physically undertaken by sifting through the oily mud hoping to spot the outline of a piece. Arriving one day on the site with the latest discriminating model which eliminated this problem, the author was able to recover numerous parts including an all-important identification tag with serial numbers which helped to identify the plane and its history. Members of the group took the important pieces home with them to restore before subsequent display in the Museum. Pieces not considered worth retaining were given to a local scrap merchant in return for the loan of his lorry. Ways and means! We recovered the engine, tailpiece, wing spar and a large part of the undercarriage.

From the information gathered it was possible to date the aircraft, a Hurricane, as approximately September 1940 from the tail wheel which, incredibly, was still partially inflated. After the dig, the research aspect really got under way with the close co-operation of the Ministry of Defence and the Imperial War Museum. It is often possible from painstakingly kept records to establish the name of the pilot or crew, his or their mission and very often through exchange of information who shot him down, whether he survived the war and much more interesting information. This has sometimes resulted in putting old wartime friends, or even adversaries, in touch with each other or in solving old mysteries. Finally, the exhibits are laid out in the Museum and attractively documented for the public to see. The displays are not always restricted to British aircraft, of course, but include German and American bombers and fighters. A Dambuster bomb, one of the famous brainchildren of Barnes Wallis, was recovered by the USAAF at Reculver's

126

testing area as only they had the necessary power to lift it with one of their 'green giant' helicopters.

Mention has been made in Chapter 7 of the valuable work done by the Bournemouth Treasure Hunters Club with the local archaeology society. This Club, together with the Hampshire Metal Detecting Club, has been instrumental in forming an association of detector clubs. Clubs throughout Britain are doing valuable work promoting responsible attitudes in metal detector users and in co-operating with the police and local charities. The Bournemouth Club has been asked to formulate a format for the Duke of Edinburgh's Award Scheme on the hobby, covering such subjects as archaeology, numismatics, geology, astronomy (affecting tides, etc) and electronics. The Club has found the following officers necessary in addition to the normal committee:

Liaison Officer—to liaise with local museums and archaeological officer

Records Officer—to record and list all coins and artefacts before sending them to the local museum

Site Arranger—to contact landowners and arrange permission including agreements on valuables found (usually 50/50)

Site Researcher—to study old maps and records before club outings are arranged

In 1977 the Club pooled its finds of coins which were handed to the Russell-Cotes Museum curator, who submitted many to the coroner for a treasure trove inquest. Significant finds included a gold Gallo-Belgic 'XB' stater, two Roman coins identified as a dupondium of Antoninius Pius (AD154) and an antoninianus of Claudius II Gothicus (AD268–270), and a silver groat of Henry VI of France minted at Calais in 1422–7.

The Ipswich Treasure Hunting Club helped the local police by searching a railway line with detectors for keys thrown away after a robbery, and metal detectors were used by police to search for the bullets fired at Princess Anne in Pall Mall in 1974.

Members of the Highland Treasure Hunters Club (*Aberdeen Journals Ltd*)

Club members and metal detectors users have done much to help local and national charities. Blind people, who so often have highly developed hearing, can get great pleasure from treasure hunting, although they do need some assistance from sighted companions; following an appeal from a blind metal detector owner in the columns of *Coin Weekly*, joint expeditions have been arranged. A metal detecting supplies shop has organised the collection of unwanted metal finds—brass, copper, corroded coins, etc—from treasure hunters; proceeds of the sale of these have been used to buy detectors for the blind. Another charitable metal detecting supplies dealer auctioned one of his more valuable finds in order to buy a wheelchair for a child suffering from spina bifida, and also organises outings to the seaside for handicapped people.

Fourteen-year-old John Yeomans of Oxford donated a Nuremburg 'Jetton' which he had found to the Oxfam Coin Appeal—the Appeal launched in 1977 for any coins, British and foreign, which had an enormous response and which no doubt profited from the finds of many detector users.

10 The Law and the Treasure Hunter

Once outside the boundary of one's own property, no person has the right to dig or search on any land without permission from the appropriate owner or authority. No more, in fact, than anyone else has the right to enter your garden and start digging holes in the lawn or moving the rockery! Some sites have a completely abandoned and desolate apperance but someone owns them and to assume otherwise could lead to early and unwelcome conflict with the law. Rule number one then: always get written permission and study bye-laws and local regulations. It is a sad fact that so often nowadays the pleasures of many are ruined by the activities of an unthinking or wilful minority. Moves to introduce legislation to seriously restrict amateur treasure hunting activities and even ownership of a detector have been largely occasioned by the undesirable actions of a few irresponsible people which, carried to extremes, could result in a shutdown of the hobby as we know it. It therefore behoves us all to behave responsibly and undoubtedly the growing influence of clubs and other organised bodies cannot fail but to do good.

The first point of law to affect the operator of a metal detector is the need to apply for and obtain a Pipe Finder/Metal Detector Licence under the Wireless Telegraphy Act 1949. The licence, which is valid for five years, currently costs £1.40 and is applied for from The Home Office, Accounts Branch, Tolworth Tower, Ewell Road, Surbiton, Surrey, KT6 7DS. Some metal detectors of foreign origin do not, however, comply with British law and their use could lead to prosecution under the Act; this should be borne in mind when choosing your detector.

The next requirement covers the reporting of finds and the law of treasure trove. There is often misunderstanding and, indeed, misapprehension when treasure trove is mentioned, but in fact the law offers protection to the treasure hunter although it contradicts the 'finders keepers' school of thought. Basically, articles containing gold or silver may be declared treasure trove if the original owner apparently hid them with the intention of returning later to reclaim them. The law is more stringent in Scotland where ancient finds of any material, including clay and base metal, are covered. Anyone finding gold or silver coins or articles made from these precious metals must at once report their finds to the local coroner through contact with the police. A receipt will of course be given. The coroner will then hold an inquest on the find to determine, if possible, the ownership of the treasure and to establish whether the treasure was deliberately hidden with a view to subsequent recovery or not. If, in the coroner's view, this was the case, but because of some circumstance such as death precluding it, then the find will be declared treasure trove and becomes the property of the Crown. It could be retained by the British Museum or other local museum, but even so, the finder would then either receive a reward equal to the value of the treasure or, in the case of a museum not requiring it, the find would be returned to him.

Fifteen-year-old Jeremy de Montfalcon and his friend Harry King unearthed a hoard of ninety-seven gold coins near Winchester. They had been searching a field but, when it started to rain, they moved into a small copse to eat their lunch. They stood up to resume their searching and Jeremy's detector immediately gave a signal; eight inches down in the leafmould Jeremy, a member of Hampshire Metal Detecting Club, found the coins neatly arranged in piles of six. There were 12 guineas dated 1773 to 1798, 2 half-guineas dated 1806 and 1810, and 83 sovereigns dated between 1817 and 1822. The find was reported to the police who in turn passed the hoard on to Dr

Kent of the British Museum. A coroner's inquest declared the find to be treasure trove and the finder's will receive their full market value—in the region of £6000 each.

There is everything to gain by reporting a find; indeed, failure to do so is a breach of the law and, far from receiving a reward, the treasure would be confiscated and a severe penalty imposed on the finder. This happened in the case of the famous Mildenhall treasure in 1946 quoted in Chapter 1 which was not reported and was reputed to be worth nearly a million pounds. Another case is that of an amateur treasure hunter from Lincolnshire who had permission from a local farmer to look for Roman pottery in his fields. He unearthed a pot containing between 15,000 and 20,000 coins dating between AD260–281. Their silver content was minute which was one reason given for not declaring the find as treasure trove. The coins were sold around the country, some for only 5p each. The finder pleaded not guilty to stealing treasure trove from the Crown, but guilty to stealing the coins from the landowner. The find was declared not to be treasure trove, but the finder was found guilty of theft and was sentenced to nine

Harry King (left) and Jeremy de Montfalcon at the coroner's inquest when their find was declared to be treasure trove

The hoard of sovereigns, guineas and half-guineas found by Harry King and Jeremy de Montfalcon

months' imprisonment, suspended for two years. Had he declared his find, he could have kept some coins and shared the full market value of the find with the landowner, instead of which further proceedings were taken by the farmer to establish his right of ownership to the coins recovered by the police.

It is often possible for the coroner to establish beyond reasonable doubt the facts surrounding the find. For instance, if a hoard of coins is found buried in a container of some kind it is pretty certain that the person or persons concealing it had every intention of returning later to recover it. The date of the coins would help to establish the period. If the coroner is quite satisfied, he will declare the find treasure trove.

The police record any finds handed in to them; if thought to be of no particular value or significance, the finder may take the item away. Otherwise, it is retained by the police and a receipt given. If not claimed within a specified time, the finder may keep it but it should be clearly understood that if the real owner subsequently turns up, he has a primary claim. It is for the finder and the owner to settle the matter between themselves. In the case of a gold or silver objects found to be of recent date, again every attempt must be made to trace the owner as the find might well be the proceeds of a burglary for example. If the owner is traced, then of course the items in question must be returned to him although the finder might receive a reward. Conversely, if the rightful owner cannot be traced, the goods would be returned to the finder in due course.

If finds are not declared treasure trove, the original owner or his heirs has the best claim to ownership, followed by the land-owner where the find was made unless the landowner has entered into a written agreement with the metal detector user. An interesting example is the case of Gary Fridd, a nine-year-old who found a 1000-year-old Saxon sword while fishing for tadpoles near his home in Yorkshire in 1976. The sword was made of iron, but bands of silver which decorated the hilt made it necessary for it to be reported to the coroner for a treasure trove inquest. It was ruled that the sword was accidentally lost or discarded by its owner, therefore it was not treasure trove and should go to Gary. The trustees of the estate which owned the banks of the stream disputed the decision but Lord Bolton, who actually owned the land and could have claimed the sword, most generously renounced his claim in Gary's favour. The sword was sold for £10,000 and is now in the Bowes Museum at Barnard Castle.

Remember also that tenants of agricultural land and build-ings have the right to be consulted. It is therefore essential to have a clearly defined agreement with the landowner regarding the ownership and disposal of any finds in order to protect all parties. Many agreements operate on a 50/50 basis. A draft agreement is given overleaf, but it is stressed that it is the responsibility of the detector user to check its validity.

In the event of a hoard being found on land where the finder did not have written permission to search, the coroner would undoubtedly award in favour of the landowner and not the finder. Ancient coins or artefacts which are made of a base metal—copper, bronze, etc—of real archaeological and historical interest should be disclosed to the local archaeological society or museum and donated if possible. If you do a lot of metal detecting in public places you are almost certain to come across small items of lost property such as rings, keys and jewellery. What you do with such things depends on their value and condition and is a question of conscience and common sense. The decent thing to do is to take them to the police station. While they may be of little value to you they could mean a lot to the loser. If such articles are not claimed by the owner within the usual time limit allowed, they will be returned to the finder. Again, do not prospect on known archaeological sites. Historical buildings and sites are usually under the protection of the Department of the Environment and penalties for non-compliance with bye-laws are prominently displayed. Ancient monuments are protected under a law of 1913.

Quite apart from the law, there are certain disciplines which we should acknowledge and obey. This is essential to safeguard the future of the hobby; some criticism is valid but much is not. However, if we follow the code of practice honestly and conscientiously we shall do much to alleviate trouble.

Public parks are fast putting up their barriers; if some of the less thoughtful treasure hunters had taken the trouble to restore the ground carefully after their operations, attitudes might well be different. The same sort of thing is happening even on beaches where some local authorities are suggesting a partial ban on treasure hunters and metal detectors. Complaints have been made about privacy being invaded and people even being asked by prospectors to move their deckchairs and belongings. To the ordinary person and respector of other people's

135

DRAFT

AN AGREEMENT
BETWEEN

.... (The Licenser)

of ....

....

.... and

.... (The Licensee)

of ....

....

....

That in consideration for .... per cent of the total value of any items that may be recovered by the Licensee, the Licenser grants permission for the property/land known as

.... to be searched by the Licensee with a metal detector subject to the following conditions being observed:

1. That all damage caused as a result of this activity is repaired by the Licensee
2. That the Licensee does not enter any enclosure containing livestock
3. That the Licensee reports any finds made to the Licenser within twenty-four hours, and reports any finds of gold or silver to the local police

Signed .... (Licenser)

Signed .... (Licensee)

Date ....

Witness ....

Address ....

....

property, the actions of the irresponsible few make one's hair stand on end but, alas, in all walks of life one comes across the cowboys.

The hobby is now beginning to assume very considerable proportions and the spotlight of publicity is increasingly being turned upon it. Sometimes the media, particularly the popular press, tend to sensationalise it—after all, if someone suddenly digs up a fortune, it is big news. Publicity, as long as it is the right kind, is a good thing, but it can tend to make a hobby or sport grow too fast and attract followers who latch on to it for the wrong reasons. Such people then start off on the wrong foot, without proper advice and experience and finish up offending the public and the authorities. This nearly happened with hang gliding, and to some extent with inexperienced and thoughtless sailors who put to sea without knowledge and caused local lifeboats to be launched. You are an ambassador for our hobby. The public will watch you with close interest when you go off to do some prospecting. Make sure that they have nothing to criticise; follow the responsible treasure hunter's code, devised by the British Amateur Treasure Hunting Club in association with the Department of the Environment.

TREASURE HUNTER'S CODE

1. Do not interfere with archaeological sites or ancient monuments. Join your local archaeological society if you are interested in ancient history.

2. Do not leave a mess. It is perfectly simple to extract a coin or other small object buried a few inches under the ground without digging a great hole. Use a sharpened trowel or knife to cut a neat circle or triangle (do not remove the plug of earth entirely from the ground); extract the object; replace the soil and grass carefully and even you will have difficulty in finding the spot again.

3. Help keep Britain tidy—and help yourself. Bottle tops, silver paper and tin cans are the last things you should throw away. You could well be digging them up again

next year. Do yourself and the community a favour by taking all the rusty junk you find to the nearest litter bin.

4. Do not trespass. Ask permission before venturing on to any private land.

5. Report all unusual historical finds to the local museum and get expert help if you accidentally discover a site of archaeological interest.

6. If you discover any live ammunition or any lethal object such as an unexploded mine, do not touch it. Mark the site clearly and report the find at once to the local police.

7. Learn the treasure trove laws and report all finds of gold and silver objects to the police. If a coroner's inquest decides that the objects were deliberately concealed with the intention of retrieving them, they become the property of the Crown and therefore treasure trove. But even it the British Museum decides to exercise its right to keep the property, the finder is granted the full market value.

8. Respect the Country Code. Do not leave gates open when crossing fields, and do not damage crops or frighten animals.

9. Never miss an opportunity to show and explain your detector to anyone who asks about it. Be friendly. You could pick up some useful clues to a good site. If you meet another detector user, introduce yourself. You may learn much about the hobby from each other.

10. Finally, remember that when you are out with your detector, you are an ambassador for the amateur hunting fraternity. Do not give us a bad name.

Further Reading

Books

Army Badges and Insignia of World War II, Guido Rosignoli
(Blandford Press)

Battlefields of Britain, The, A. H. Burne (Methuen)

Battles in Britain 1642–1746, William Seymour (Sidgwick &
Jackson)

Battles of the English Civil War, Austin Woolrych (Pan)

Book of the Seaside (Drive Publications)

British Coins 1816–1969 (Seaby)

British Tokens and Their Values (Seaby)

Buried & Sunken Treasure (Marshall Cavendish)

Coin 1977 Year Book (Numismatic Publishing Co)

Coin Collecting, P. Frank Purvey (Seaby)

Coin Hoards of Great Britain and Ireland, D. I. Brown & Michael
Dolly (Royal Numismatic Society)

Detective in the Landscape: In South East England, Marcus Crouch
(Longman Young Books)

Dictionary of Battles, Thomas Harbottle (Hart-Davis)

Dictionary of Battles from 1479BC to the Present, David Eggenberger
(Allen & Unwin)

Dowsing, Tom Graves (Turnstone Press)

Encyclopaedia of Antiques, George Savage (Barrie & Jenkins)

English Copper, Tin and Bronze Coins 1558–1958, C. Wilson-Peck
(British Museum)

English Field Names, John Field (David & Charles)

English Place Names and Their Origins, G. J. Copley (David &
Charles)

Fortune Hunters' Guide, The, Peter Haining (Sidgwick & Jackson)

Goodwin Sands Shipwrecks, Richard Larn (David & Charles)
Hidden Treasure, S. C. George (David & Charles)
Infantry Uniforms, Latham & Latham (Blandford Press)
Landscape Archaeology, Michael Aston & Trevor Rowley (David & Charles)
Military Roads in Scotland, William Taylor (David & Charles)
No Through Road (Drive Publications)
Pewter Collector, The, H. J. L. J. Massé (Barrie & Jenkins)
Reed's Nautical Almanack (Reed)
Regimental Badges, T. J. Edwards (Charles Knight)
Roman Coins and Their Values (Seaby)
Sutton Hoo Ship Burial, The, Rupert Bruce-Mitford (British Museum)
Tomb of Tutankhamen, The, Howard Carter (Sphere Books)
Treasure Hunting, Edward Fletcher (MAB Publications)
Treasure Hunting For All, Edward Fletcher (Blandford Press)
Treasure and Treasure Hunters, ed Richard Armstrong (Hamish Hamilton)
Treasures of the Armada, Robert Stenuit (David & Charles)
Treasures of Britain (Drive Publications)

Booklets

The Large Scale County Maps of the British Isles, E. M. Rodger (Bodleian Library)
Maps for the Local Historian, J. B. Harley (National Council of Social Service)

Maps

First Edition of the One Inch Ordnance Survey Maps (David & Charles)
Special Ordnance Survey Maps: *Britain in the Dark Ages*
Roman Britain
Iron Age Britain

Periodicals

Coin Monthly
Gemcraft
Search
Treasure Hunting

Index

(pages on which relevant illustrations appear are indicated by *italics*)